THE DISCIPLE SHIP

A Practical Understanding of Discipleship

By James Arceneaux Jr.

Published By TAG Publishing

TAG THE COMPANY

thearceneauxgroup@yahoo.com

Scriptures attained from the Easy-to-Read Version at biblegateway.com.
Illustrations and design by
James Arceneaux and Leslie Moffett
Cover by: wwwButterflyGrafix.com

Library of Congress
Cataloging-in-Publication Data:
ISBN Number: 978-0-9851618-6-6

Executive Editor
Cynthia Pineda, Ph.D.

Editors
Lorna Constance
Leslie Moffett

Compiled by
James Arceneaux, Jr.
Vernon Lynch, Jr.

Published by
The Arceneaux Group

Format and interior design BY
SPAN: Self Published Authors Network

Published By TAG Publishing

Dedication

I dedicate this work of love to Jesus Christ
and to all those who, like myself,
dedicated their hearts to the Lord
and remained lost at sea.
May this book steer you to
the Kingdom of Heaven,
once and for all.

Foreword

The Disciple Ship reminds me of the golf course where I first heard about this book. During our rounds, James wouldn't stop talking about discipleship. No matter the day or time, the conversation was the same. Discipleship this, discipleship that. Finally, one day I said, "Dude, write a book about it so you can stop talking and start playing!" Soon after, he handed me this book.

James is a passionate disciple. His aim, no matter the environment, is to win souls. The Disciple Ship is a beautiful witness of a man's obedience to The Lord Jesus Christ. There is no doubt Jesus is involved in this book. Read and see for yourself.

As the Pastor of In His Presence Church in Woodland Hills California, I've read many books and met many people. Over the years, I've gotten to know James personally and there's one thing I know for sure: James is a disciple with a purpose. I've not only read his book; I've read the man. I've watched James in action, both inside and outside of church, and no matter where he is or whom he's with, James disciples. This kind of passion is found deep in the heart of a love for Jesus, a love for souls, a love for His Kingdom, and a love for today's church to disciple those who come to the Lord.

The beauty of The Disciple Ship is this: whether you're a new believer or a seasoned disciple, you'll feel the desire to get closer to Jesus. The Disciple Ship instructs us to disciple souls who want to grow deeper in their faith in Jesus Christ. This book provides answers to questions we all encounter in our walk with Christ.

Reading and studying The Disciple Ship equips you to disciple future disciples while simultaneously strengthening your own faith.

Over the years, James and I have challenged one another in a game we both love. It's no secret I can outdrive him in golf—even he admits it—but I couldn't have come close to writing a better discipleship book.

The Disciple Ship should be in the hands of every pastor, prayer counselor and congregation member and on the shelves of every church bookstore. It deepens the knowledge and understanding of God's Word for new believers and church leaders alike, making it the ideal read for anyone looking for Biblical answers to common questions. Most importantly, what we learn from reading The Disciple Ship will make us stronger, more confident, better prepared disciples. After reading this book, we will look every sinner in the eyes who comes to Christ and say, "Welcome aboard."

Mel Ayers, Pastor

In His Presence Church

Editor's Note

I received my first Bible when I was 29 years of age. Prior to that, I didn't know anything about God. "Religion," my father would say, "is a form of social control." In our home, there was no such thing as God—much less any super hero named Jesus.

I lived my life thinking religion was for the weak and gullible. Then, when I least expected it, my life took a drastic turn, and for the first time ever, I sought solace in a higher being. In search of answers, I turned to books. I read everything from New Age to Neuroscience, but nothing, absolutely nothing, soothed my soul. On the one hand, I felt a nagging need to fill a void, but on the other, I didn't know how to fill it.

Part frustration, part curiosity, I did the unthinkable—I reached for a Bible. I was instantly intimidated. I'm an avid reader, but nothing could've prepared me for this book. With no guidance whatsoever, I opened the Bible and began reading from page one in the Book of Genesis.

After months of aimless reading, I met James. We talked about God and the Bible. James couldn't help but laugh at my efforts to intellectualize God. "James," I said, defending my position, "I have to understand God before I can trust God." James chuckled. "Read this," he said, handing me a manuscript, "Then tell me what you think." Little did I know this document would change my life. I finished the manuscript and sent James an email. Below is an excerpt:

As you well know, there's resistance on my part to accept Jesus. In my mind, I'd make the final decision AFTER

I read the bible. I know you're probably laughing

at me right now…

Last night though, I prayed for Jesus to come into my life. I asked him to forgive me, fill me with his spirit and be my Lord and Savior.

I wouldn't have done that last night if it wasn't for you and your book. As I edit, I search the Bible for accuracy. Thanks to your book, I've read scriptures that I wouldn't have gotten to for months. I've come to the conclusion that I don't need to read the entire bible to believe in Jesus. Sure, I will continue to read and learn. But I'm done second-guessing.

The Disciple Ship taught me a valuable lesson: understanding comes after trust in God, not the other way around. Today, this skeptic knows one thing for sure: God lives, not in our heads, but in our hearts.

Bon Voyage,
Cynthia Pineda, Ph.D.

Contents

Preface

Welcome aboard The Disciple Ship. Whether you're a new believer or a seasoned disciple, I welcome you on this journey to the Kingdom of Heaven. Here you will find Biblical truths in a simple and straightforward manner. The thoughts and principles shared in this book will help you walk with God in faith and depend on Him alone.

One reoccurring theme in this book is questions. While this book provides answers to several questions, I urge you to ask God questions of your own. Here you will learn how to ask God questions, and most importantly, how to listen to God's responses. God knows you and your needs, he knows you search daily for the purpose and meaning to life. He knows the answers to questions you have yet to ask.

The Disciple Ship is designed to strengthen your relationship with God and should complement your daily reading of the Bible. After all, the Bible can be used without reading this book, but this book has no value without the Bible. Therefore, open your mind, heart and Bible as you read along. Begin with prayer to allow God to speak to you as He's done throughout time to those who desire to hear Him.

I wrote The Disciple Ship to address an unfortunate truth—new believers of the Christian faith, after giving their hearts to the Lord, are sent home with little to no discipleship. Without a mature believer to explain and display how to be a true child of God, new believers become discouraged and disheartened. I know this from personal experience.

I was 13 years old when I first received Jesus Christ as my Lord and Savior. It was a time when many of my friends were getting baptized. I didn't quite understand what baptism meant, but I went

along with it anyway. At least I'd make my parents proud, I reasoned.
When the ceremony ended and the celebration was over, I went home wondering how my life would now be different. In the innocence of my youth, I imagined my pastor visiting my home to have long talks with me about being a Christian and church leaders guiding my path as a new believer. But no one from that church reached out to me, not a single individual. With no mentorship in sight, I grew to recognize baptism as nothing more than an empty, meaningless Christian ritual. A great deal of disappointment filled my heart and I returned to my old ways of sinning.

Later in my adult life, while attending church, I answered an altar call and confessed Jesus Christ as my Lord and Savior. This time would be different, I reasoned, because I was older and wiser. Newly baptized, again I imagined an outpour of love from members of my church. The prayer counselor who promised to contact me after my altar call would contact me, I thought. He would be the one to see if I was going back to my old ways. But much to my dismay, I never received the call I anxiously awaited.

As days turned into weeks, I realized neither he nor anyone else was going to contact me. I yearned for direction and guidance as a new believer. I needed someone to answer my questions, someone to model after, someone to ask if I was making prayer an active part of my life, someone to check if I was reading the Word of God, someone to look for me Sunday mornings. Simply put, I needed a disciple. The truth is, we all need discipleship; the unfortunate truth is some of us don't receive it.

Reading The Disciple Ship affirms your commitment to being discipled and discipling others. Of course, becoming a disciple of Jesus Christ means more than just reading this book, or any other book. It involves the pouring of your life into the lives of others as you receive new revelations from the Lord.

As God continuously pours into your life, I encourage you to share His love, grace, mercy, and truth with everyone you know. The ultimate offering is your life in service to Christ. You will see that your growth and maturity in the Lord does not come as a result of what you receive from the Lord, but rather what you give. ***Welcome aboard The Disciple Ship.***

Acknowledgements

I extend my profound love and gratitude to those who influenced this project. It is because of your unwavering commitment to the ministry of the Lord and your passion to see lives transformed by God's Word that this work has come to its completion.

I would like to give special thanks to the Following people: Carla Kennedy, Jay Williams, Johnny Mack, Jerry & Tamiko Mosely, The Murphy Family, The Clarkson Family, Skip James Mullen, Robert Ross, Chuck Wilson, Gerald Honeywell, Lisa Harrington.

Thank you to all who helped give life to God's word, especially Vernon Lynch Jr., Wayne Lewis, Greg Dalton, Dennis Dodd, Richard T. and Nancy Jones, Rosie Patterson, Al Scaife, , Leslie Moffett, David Munyer, Darryl Heath, Pamela Mougin, Kyndel Jones, , Nicole Haynes and Sharon Arceneaux. Johnny Gill your friendship has been a blessing beyond belief, thank you my friend.

The real work, whether producing a movie, recording music or writing a book, takes place in the editing process. Dr. Cynthia Pineda and Lorna Constance, your work as editors is amazing and allows this book to flow in the Spirit.

I humbly thank all of the members of In His Presence Church and most of all, Pastor Mel Ayers who inspired me through a conversation on the golf course to write The Disciple Ship. Andre Dawson, thanks for lifting me up during tough times, you have no idea what you did for me., Chris and Vanessa Spencer thank you for your support. Darnell, Anthony and Justin my three sons, I love you and your families.

My loving and thoughtful sister Lisa Arceneaux, you have been an amazing inspiration and an awesome sister. Thank you for leading our family's list of dedicated evangelists. Mom and Dad, what a joy it is to have you both still here, happy and healthy, I love you. Both of you are amazing people in my life. I'm so grateful that you listened to the heart of God and gave me back to Him. If I've forgotten anyone, please find it in your heart to forgive me.

Today I challenge those of you who say you love the Lord and want to become one of His disciples. I challenge you to dedicate the rest of your lives to God and to filling up the Kingdom of Heaven with the lost souls of this world. We who say we love God should make every effort to be absolutely sure that those who express their faith and put their belief in the Lord Jesus Christ have an understanding of who He is, their God-given purpose and destiny, and without a doubt, commit to never leaving His presence. I pray to the Lord that from this day on, I will be a leader and a visible example of discipleship.

TRANSFORMED BY JESUS

Introduction—TESTIFY

"So go and make followers of all people in the world. Baptize them in the name of the Father and the Son and the Holy Spirit. Teach them to obey everything that I have told you to do. You can be sure that I will be with you always. I will continue with you until the end of time"

(Matthew 28:18-20)

My Testimony

The morning of April 22, 2001 was a turning point in my life. I'd just gotten out of a seven-year relationship with a woman, and now that our relationship was over, my life was a disaster zone. It was as if a freight train collided with my plans and dreams. I was a sinking ship in troubled waters.

Everything I knew and loved was scattered all around me: my finances, my job and my home. Everything was in shambles. The only thing I recognized was my heart, and that too was broken. I was by myself and had nothing to stand on and no one to believe in. God truly had me just where He wanted—alone.

I'd been living the good life and was quite an arrogant guy. I enjoyed all the luxuries that my work in the entertainment business had to offer: disposable income, designer clothes, extravagant parties, and beautiful women. I received praise from high profile entertainers I worked with and was well respected for never drinking alcohol or using drugs. I traveled around the globe, visited the most exotic places and met some of the most influential people in the world. But nothing, absolutely nothing, could heal the brokenness I felt inside.

To make matters worse, I was blinded by the fact that I was never "down and out." I was "up and out." What's the difference, you ask? Pride. Despite my growing ego, God never left my side. In fact, God was reaching out to me through my friend and well-known actor in the entertainment business, Flex Alexander.

Flex called every Sunday morning to invite me to church. Most of the time, I ignored his calls. But every once in a while, I'd answer, hoping he wanted to talk about something, anything, other than church. To my disappointment, his calls were always an invitation to service.

I'd say I was already on my way, then hang up and go right back to sleep. Sometimes he'd surprise me and call Sunday evenings. "I sat in the back," I'd say, hoping he wouldn't ask any follow-up questions.

But the truth is, I was lying. I had no intentions of attending church. You see, I'd tried the church thing once before and it did nothing for me. Church disappointed me and it hardened my heart, and as a result, I couldn't hear God's voice. Bitterness, hurt, anger, and pride were the culprits. I bolted out of God's loving arms and ran into the seducing arms of the enemy. And what a mess he made of my life.

Although I didn't realize it at the time, God was present all along. He was reaching out to me, but I was blinded by my desire to be my own God. My ways blocked my view of His helping hand. I, like so many, depended on the world to fill a void and was now suffering the consequences. I was a miserable, lonesome wreck.

That is, until Sunday morning, April 22, 2001. I was in bed, relieved to be off my feet after a hectic Hollywood night. It was nearly 3:00AM. I was exhausted and anxious to sleep, but my mind and body were restless. I looked at the digital clock every now and again, each time more frustrated than the last for time wasted on tossing and turning.

Just as I was drifting off to sleep, I felt a touch on my shoulder and heard a whisper in my ear. The words were loud and clear, "In the name of Jesus." The touch and words were simultaneous and spontaneous. It felt and heard so human that I opened my eyes expecting to attack the intruder. I jolted out of bed and searched the room, but I was home alone. Who touched me? Who spoke those words? I still don't know. But that moment changed my life.

The next morning I woke up just in time to attend the 11:00AM service. I got dressed and called Flex to tell him I was coming to church. He wasn't so convinced since I lied so many times before, but I told him I was serious this time.

When I arrived, I chose a seat in the back and listened to the Word of God. I had no clue what the message was about, I just knew I had to be present. I sat and listened patiently. I believed God was waiting on me and I didn't want to disappoint Him. When the altar call began, I felt a sense of relief and tears flowed down my face. I hurried out of my seat, humbly walked to the front and willingly gave my broken heart to the Lord.

Of all the times I'd done an altar call before, this time was real. I was converted—once and for all. I was saved, glory to God! My search was finally over. God was now poised to restore what the world had damaged.

At the alter call, one of the pastors noticed my tears. He handed me his handkerchief, "Keep it," he said. I wiped my tears and wrote on it, "April 22, 2001—1PM I gave my heart to the Lord and on this handkerchief are the tears of my sincerity." To this day, I carry the handkerchief in my Bible.

My Calling

The next morning, Monday, April 23, 2001, I went to the local Bible bookstore. I bought just about every book that mentioned Jesus or the Bible; I bought Bible concordances, study books, discipleship books, and books on how to study the Bible. I was eager to learn about God, Jesus and His Word.

As I walked out of the bookstore, I noticed a young lady crying on the curb. I kneeled down, smiled and tried to console her, but to no avail. "My life's crazy," she whimpered, "I don't know what to do." At a loss for words, I handed her a Bible I purchased just minutes ago. "Read this," I told her, "There's information in here that'll help you." After that encounter, I knew my life purpose was to win souls for the Lord.

That day, I made a promise to the Lord. The next time I met someone in need of help or in search of God, I would have answers. I began to study the Bible with passion and purpose. I prayed, studied the Word, prayed again, and studied the Word some more. This became my daily routine. Anyone I encountered heard about my love for the Lord. I told them who I was before I met Him, what changes He made in my life, and how He'd change them too, if they accepted Him into their lives.

One day in prayer, I asked God for guidance on how to help people who were hurting, especially my friends in the entertainment business. God told me to study His Word and be prepared to have answers for those who were seeking the truth. He also told me prayer was an important aspect of loving people and that I should pray for those I wished to help.

With God's guidance, I formed an organization named R.E.A.P., Remembering Entertainers and Athletes in Prayer. The function of this organization was to pray for entertainers and professional athletes all over the world. Every Sunday morning at 6:00AM, R.E.A.P. members prayed. The prayer group fueled my passion for serving the Lord. When the organization discontinued, I immediately began thinking of other ways to serve.

A good friend of mine, actor TK Carter, recommended I start a Bible study in my home. "You can learn about the Lord with other believers," TK suggested. I hesitated because my apartment was too small, but TK insisted, "Ask God for a bigger place." I followed his advice and prayed. I promised God that if my prayer was answered, I'd use the space to host weekly Bible study. Sure enough, a week after my prayer request, I received the keys to a bigger apartment for nearly the same price. Hallelujah!

Right after I moved in to my new apartment, I started my Bible study group, just as I promised the Lord. During that time, my friend Daryl Heath said, "The Lord instructed me to disciple you." I knew Daryl for some time, but I had no idea what he knew about the Lord. Boy was I in for a blessing of a lifetime. My discipleship experience began and my life transformed.

My Discipleship

Daryl and I started our discipleship process by conducting weekly Bible studies in my home. I was the host and Daryl served as the group moderator and leader. At first, not a lot of people attended. People expressed interest when we invited them over, but their interest quickly faded when we uttered the words "Bible study."

After some prayer and discussion, Daryl and I decided to call our weekly meeting a "Bible discussion group." We described it as a meeting where people from all walks of life shared their understanding of the Bible, their relationship with God, and their application of the Word of God in real life situations.

Sure enough, the shift in language appealed to a larger audience and to our delight, attendance increased. Mothers sent their children, children brought their parents, we invited our neighbors, and strangers looking for answers to life's tough questions all showed up to receive God's love.

At one point, people who knew me before I rededicated my life to Christ questioned my sincerity. "Bible study?" some asked, "Is this dude serious?" But whispers of doubt faded when they heard the success stories from members of the group. People were experiencing so much intrapersonal change that we started calling my apartment the "self-examination room." It became so popular, even the naysayers wanted to join.

Daryl was a superb disciple. He knew the Word, and best of all, he knew how to translate it in practical terms. I was so astonished at how well Daryl understood and explained the Bible. Each time we went out to share the gospel, he amazed me. He'd take the most hardened heart and soften it with a dose of love and truth. I remember telling God one day, "Lord, I want some of what he's got!"

Daryl wasn't only a worker for the Lord, he was also my teacher, friend and accountability partner. Over the course of four years, we were together almost every single day. We watched movies together and discussed how Jesus would perceive the film. We attended dinner parties and social events. We went to the gym. We watched the news. We became real close friends. He checked on my personal life and asked how my kids and family were doing, how I was feeling that day, how my job was going, who I was dating, and if I was being sexual with any women. Nothing was off-limits for Daryl.

After a while, everyone knew we were the two guys who always discussed the Lord. No matter where we were, we started a dialogue to reel people into our conversation. At the local gym, we were known as the "sauna preachers." We discussed anything and everything and it worked like a charm. Daryl knew exactly how to lead people to the Lord. He shared his testimony and his personal experiences. Then, he persuaded people with the Word of God by making it so simple, anyone from any age, religion or background would relate.

Daryl spoke of the Lord and made it fun for everyone. You see, Daryl was not only an amazing disciple, he was also a talented comedian. He believed Jesus was a comedian too, since the Lord experiences all things. "Imagine," Daryl would say, "Jesus must've been so funny that the disciples laughed their heads off." He's probably right. Daryl too used a great deal of humor. No matter where we went, we had a crowd around us laughing while learning about Christ.

As I watched Daryl disciple, I learned to disciple as well. Daryl had a gift for talking to people. He corrected me when I made mistakes. He showed me how to get people to open their hearts. He showed me how to pray for people. He showed me how to share the gospel. He taught me how to be a faithful tither. Daryl taught me how to be a disciple. He spoke into my life and gave of himself. He made himself available, no matter what was going on in his life. He carried God's capacity for the kingdom. He loved me and made sure I received the gospel God purposed for all men and women. He was truly God's man. He believed the Lord could fix the worst of human conditions and was the most hopeful person I ever met.

Thanks to Daryl, I learned the true meaning of discipleship. It doesn't matter it took me 42 years to get to this point—what matters is I received Christ as my Lord and Savior, once and for all. I tried in my teens and later in my 20s, but each attempt ended in disappointment. The difference this time was discipleship. I've traveled the world and never met another person like Daryl. Daryl was a brother in Christ who took a personal interest in my walk with the Lord. Quite simply, Daryl cared. We prayed daily. We studied the Word of God together. He answered my questions. Finally, after so many years in search of God, I was at peace. Through discipleship, I began to experience victories in areas of insecurities, weaknesses and deficiencies.

For the first time in my life, thanks to the incredible discipleship I received from Daryl, I left behind my 'net' of self-dependency, sufficiency and self-gratification. I learned to put all my faith in God. When I recommitted my heart to the Lord, my life changed forever. I've been filled with the power of God's Spirit ever since. I'm grateful every day that I gave my heart to the Lord. Christ is now everything to me. He's everything I am and everything I live for. Being discipled was the most amazing experience of my life.

Daryl remains alive and well in my heart. As I avail myself to be used of God, I pray to win souls for Christ and be a positive and continuous witness in the life of a new believer.

Part I—DISCIPLE

"Come, follow me, and I will make you
a different kind of fishermen.
You will bring in people, not fish"
(Matthew 4:19)

Who is a disciple?

Generally speaking, a disciple is a follower. When you hear the word "follower," perhaps you think of a submissive, passive or easily influenced person. But in the Christian faith, a disciple is a different kind of follower. When we speak of a disciple, we refer to a spiritually mature believer who (1) possesses unquestionable faith that Jesus is the Son of God, (2) models his or her life after the teaching of Jesus, and (3) provides guidance and training in God's Word to others. In essence, a disciple is a teacher of Christ.

You can think of a disciple as a teacher; the Bible as the

curriculum; the world as the classroom; human beings as the students; and heaven as the graduation ceremony. A disciple, no matter how spiritually mature he or she is, is both a teacher and a student. In this classroom, there is always room for growth. God, the Creator of the Universe, is the only one who knows everything, that's why God is omniscient. The rest of us, including the most spiritually mature disciples, must continue to learn and grow to become more like Christ.

What is discipleship?

Discipleship is the act of teaching someone how to study, obey and apply God's Word. This process includes a spiritually mature believer, often called a disciple, mentor or teacher, who provides loving guidance and training in God's Word to an individual. This individual, often called a disciplee, mentee or student, is someone with a teachable spirit who desires to learn about Jesus and the Christian faith. With time and effort, disciplees becomes disciplers and efforts are multiplied.

The discipleship process is an intentional and purposeful effort to obey God. In fact, discipleship is not for a select few; rather, God commands all believers to disciple. Consider what Jesus told his disciples, "So he came to them and said, 'All authority in heaven and on earth is given to me. So go and make followers of all people in the world. Baptize them in the name of the Father and the Son and the Holy Spirit. Teach them to obey everything that I have told you to do. You can be sure that I will be with you always. I will continue with you until the end of time'" (***Matthew***

28:18-20). All believers are called by God to create followers of Jesus, but before a believer begins discipling, he or she must be discipled first.

How did discipleship begin?

The Bible describes how God's Son, Jesus, began discipling:

Jesus was walking by Lake Galilee. He saw Simon and his brother Andrew. These two men were fisherman, and they were throwing a net into the lake to catch fish. Jesus said to them, "Come, follow me, and I will make you a different kind of fisherman. You will bring in people, not fish." So they immediately left their nets and followed Jesus. Jesus continued walking by Lake Galilee. He saw two more brothers, James and John, the sons of Zebedee. They were in their boat, preparing their nets to catch fish. Their father Zebedee and the men who worked for him were in the boat with the brothers. When Jesus saw the brothers, he told them to come. They left their father and followed Jesus (***Mark 1:16-20***).

Who did Jesus disciple?

The Bible describes who Jesus discipled:

Then Jesus went up on a hill and invited those he wanted to go with him. So they joined him there. And he chose twelve men and called them apostles. He wanted these twelve men to be with him, and he wanted to send them to other places to tell people God's message. He also wanted them to have the power to force demons out of people. These are the names of the twelve men Jesus chose:

- Simon (the one Jesus named Peter),
- James and his brother John, the sons of Zebedee (the ones Jesus named Boanerges, which means "Sons of Thunder"),
- Andrew
- Phillip
- Bartholomew
- Matthew
- Thomas
- James, the son of Alphaeus
- Thaddaeus
- Simon, the Zealot
- Judas Iscariot (the one who handed Jesus over to his enemies)
  (**Mark 3:13-19**).

How did Jesus disciple?

Jesus had a strategy. He spent three years with his disciples. His objective was to bear witnesses to his life and carry on His work. He used men as His method. He didn't use information, tradition or religion. Rather, he used honest, ordinary men who were willing to learn and dedicate their lives to Jesus. Many of them didn't have much formal education or training. These men were ordinary people like you and me. They were temperamental, prejudiced, and at times, fearful—not the kind of people you'd expect to win souls for the Lord, yet they became superb disciples because they received superb discipleship.

How do I identify a disciple?

Daryl's discipleship was a blessing. He gave of himself so willingly and selflessly. Unfortunately, not all Christians disciple like Daryl. "Remember," Daryl would say, "not all Christians are the same." Since some believers are more spiritually mature than others, we need a way to identify the disciples. To do this, Daryl developed four easy-to-remember categories: The Christian, The Believer, The Follower, and The Disciple.

The Christian: "Christians" believe in God, Jesus and the Holy Spirit. They give their life to the Lord; but they put God in their picture instead of being in His. They attend church occasionally, pray sporadically and don't study the Word of God. They do not know much about how to live as a believer and often lack faith in God.

The Believer: "Believers" give their life to the Lord, attend church regularly and read the Bible from time to time. They attempt to share the gospel and love their neighbors. They invite people to church occasionally, but they're not too concerned with growing in the Lord. They may repeat sermons and scriptures, but rarely give testimony to match God's word.

The Follower: "Followers" give their life to the Lord, attend church weekly, tithe regularly, and serve in ministry. If the opportunity presents itself, they lead people to the Lord. They have a genuine interest in the study and application of the Bible, but not necessarily with a purpose. They desire to do God's will and are capable of becoming a disciple, but fall short. They may be holding onto a few things in the world they feel guilty about, preventing them from fully connecting to God.

The Disciple: "Disciples" hear a call to follow Jesus. They give their entire lives to God and have absolute, unquestionable faith in Him. They never compromise in the areas of tithing, soul winning, worship, prayer, ministry, and studying and defending the gospel. They're determined to obey and please God in all areas of their lives. They know God's word and are willing to give their lives for God. They refer to scriptures, lead souls to the Lord, attend church religiously, invite people regularly, and seek new believers to disciple.

How long does discipleship take?

Discipleship is not a weekend or Sunday experience, it's a continuous process that's always in session. Think of true discipleship as a life-long process. It takes time and commitment to disciple someone and to be discipled. For discipleship to be effective, a disciple must be willing to share their time. Disciples should show disciplees how to obey God, how to grow in the Word, how to pray daily, and how to disciple others.

A disciple must be focused and intentional about nurturing in the faith. Discipleship is a learning process that requires time and patience. Therefore, the student and the teacher should discuss time commitments and expectations. From personal experience, I've learned that a multi-year discipleship experience is especially beneficial for the student, though not mandatory.

How soon should discipleship begin?

Every time an individual places their entire lives in the hands of God, there's a great celebration. The heavenly host and angels—seraphim and cherubim—praise our victories over sin. Those of us on earth who witness this supernatural and life-changing event celebrate as well. There's no greater victory in heaven and on earth than the saving of a soul. But before we get too excited, we must remember that what happens after an individual gives their heart to the Lord is as important as the event itself. In fact, what I learned from my own conversion experience is that when an individual accepts Jesus Christ as their Lord and Savior, discipleship must begin immediately. Why? The very moment one receives Jesus into their lives, they're willing and ready to be discipled—right then and there.

A born-again believer experiences much joy and excitement about their new life in Christ. They want to follow Jesus, hear stories of other followers and learn about the Christian faith. During this exciting transition, many new believers are invited to become members of their local church, and that's great, but a newborn believer can never be satisfied with just a Sunday serving of Jesus. A new believer wants and needs more of Him. A new believer becomes keenly aware of the abundant resources available in Him and has a curiosity to know what they are and how to appropriate them in their lives.

You see, a newborn believer in the faith has a thirst for God and His word. Much like a newborn babe who desires its mother's milk, a newborn believer thirsts as well, but for spiritual milk. Consider the following scripture, "Like newborn babies hungry for milk, you should want the pure teaching that feeds your spirit. With it you can grow up and be saved" (***1 Peter 2:2***). If this thirst for God and His Word is not immediately quenched, it'll be replaced and satisfied by worldly desires and enticements...and we all know where that leads. Therefore, a newborn believer must be discipled immediately by someone willing to nurture their spiritual growth as Daryl did for me.

Part II – BELIEVE

"Without faith no one can please God.
Whoever comes to God must believe that he is real
and that he rewards those who sincerely try to find him"
(Hebrews 11:6)

Where is your home?

Long ago, God built a beautiful home made of gold, pearl and onyx. This beautiful home was a wonder to the imagination. By today's standards, people around the world would pay to see it with their own eyes.

This home had everything anyone could ever desire. God named this home Eden and is described in the book of Genesis, "Then the Lord God planted a garden in the East, in a place named Eden. He put the man he made in that garden. Then the Lord God caused all the beautiful trees that were good for food to grow in the garden. In the middle of the garden, he put the tree of life and the tree that gives knowledge about good and evil" (***Genesis 2:8-9***). God gave man dominion over this home and everything in it, including the entire animal kingdom.

Unfortunately, man did not appreciate this home. How do we know this? In the book of Genesis, scripture tells us man lost his rights to the home, "God forced the man to leave the garden. Then he put Cherub angels and a sword of fire at the entrance to the garden to protect it. The sword flashed around and around, guarding the way to the tree of life" (***Genesis 3:24***). The penalties for disobeying God left man homeless, EVICTED BY GOD HIMSELF.

To be homeless is a serious matter, and unless you want to remain homeless, you must decide on a plan of action. Some choose to obey God and have a born-again relationship with Christ. This pleases God and He welcomes them back home. Others, however, remain homeless because they choose to disobey and disbelieve God.

God wants you to return home—the home he created for you—regardless of what you've done in the past. Why? Because He's rich in love, grace, mercy, and forgiveness. All He asks you to do is have faith. He wants you to believe He sent His one and only unique son Jesus to pay the penalty for our eviction and He wants you to obey His Word. When you believe and obey, you receive eternal spiritual life and heaven becomes your home once again.

Who is Your (Land) Lord?

Jesus does not offer eternal life based on anything you say or do. Rather, eternal life is based on faith in, and obedience of, God's

Word. Your belief in and confession of Jesus Christ as your Lord and Savior activates your conversion. Conversion, you ask, what does that mean? Conversion means that the very moment you express faith in Christ and confess him to be your Lord and Savior, a miraculous change occurs. The 'old person' who did not please God or obey His commandments is replaced with the 'new person' in Christ. This conversion frees you from the bondage of sin, cleanses you from all unrighteous, and gives you eternal life in heaven. Feelings of guilt, shame, disappointment, and anger are replaced with love, joy and peace. In following Christ, you gain an intimate relationship with God. In this relationship, you encounter God's power and understand His will, purpose, provision, and desires for your life. As you draw closer and closer to God, you gain full access to the abundant life only He can provide.

Your inner life, once formed by immoral beliefs and practices, are changed into the image of Christ…hallelujah! Inner change is a work of the Spirit of grace. It cannot be accomplished through mere human power, will or determination. The Bible provides the following advice on this conversion process, "Don't change yourselves to be like the people of this world, but let God change you inside with a new way of thinking. Then you will be able to understand and accept what God wants for you. You will be able to know what is good and pleasing to him and what is perfect" (***Romans 12:2***). Put your trust in God, seek His guidance, allow Him to sit on the throne of your heart, and witness the miracles occur in your life. Belief in God will direct, restore and sustain you now and for eternity.

While your faith in God saves you from sin, it does not prevent the temptation to sin. Consider this verse, "Surely you know that you become the slaves of whatever you give yourselves to. Anything or anyone you follow will be your master. You can follow sin, or you can obey God. Following sin brings spiritual death, but obeying God makes you right with him" (***Romans 6:16***). Every day you must decide whether to obey or disobey God. When you make a conscious and continuous effort to obey God's Word and you pray for God's guidance, you'll overcome any temptation.

If, for any reason you dishonor God, don't beat yourself up or give up on God. Instead, pray to God, repent of your action, seek His forgiveness, and rededicate your life to Him. Rest assured, God will accept and forgive you. Because of your repentance, God will throw your sins into the sea of forgetfulness and you'll no longer be considered a sinner. If you don't know what to say in prayer, read the Rededication Prayer written for you at the end of this book. It's what I prayed when I rededicated my life to the Lord. Feel free to change the words to fit your situation.

The living of your faith is the only way to validate the powerful work of Christ in you. As you grow to learn what pleases God, conduct your life in a manner that's worthy of the Gospel of Christ. With the help of the Holy Spirit, you'll live a victorious Christian life. Practice the spiritual disciplines of prayer, fasting, meditation, Bible reading, tithing, offering, worship, evangelism, service, and fellowship with other believers. With time, you'll grow into a spiritually mature disciple who leads others to Christ.

What are the house rules?

Your acceptance of Christ immediately reconciles you to God and makes you a member of the most spiritually dynamic team ever, God's family. Whether you confessed Christ as your Lord and Savior just seconds ago or you've been walking with the Lord all your life, you play an important role in this home. As a member, you're expected to pray to God and obey His Word. These are house rules.

God desires we all spend time with Him. We receive specific instruction in Jeremiah 33:3, "Judah, pray to mc, and I will answer you. I will tell you important secrets. You have never heard these things before." God answers questions as you spend time with Him in prayer. When you begin to do so, you will soon find yourself drawing closer and closer to the Lord.

An intimate relationship with Christ is so rewarding. He teaches you His ways, reveals the wonderful plans He has for your life, and provides strength, protection, leadership, and guidance. Over time, you lose your dependency on this world and learn to depend on God.

You develop such a close relationship with Him that He becomes your best friend. After all, He knows everything about you, from the number of hairs on your head to the number of tears you've cried. He knows your hidden secrets, burdens, pain, regrets, longings, desires, and cares. No one else can ever claim such knowledge of you. He's waiting to hear your prayer.

A great way to begin prayer is to say, "Father in Heaven." You see, there is only one God in Heaven, so when you say that, He knows you're addressing Him specifically. To cultivate an active, fruitful, and exciting prayer life, pray every day. Yes, every day. Prayer is not an option, but a command from God.

You have complete access to God so make full use of it. Pray anytime, anywhere. God is never too busy or too tired to hear your voice. You have the right and privilege, as a child of God, to go before Him and share your fears, desires, joys, achievements, and most intimate thoughts. Nothing is off-limits to God and absolutely everything about you is important to Him.

The Word of God is our spiritual food. Just as your physical body needs food and water for existence, your spirit needs food too. Although this "food" isn't edible, it's necessary for you to stay connected to the Divine power-source. Poor diet results in severe malnutrition. The Bible has all the spiritual nutrients we need so study the Word. Make a conscious effort to have a daily intake of the Word of God.

Think of the Bible as the Basic Instructions Before Leaving Earth. God speaks to us through His Word. He tells us who He is, what He's done, and what He'll do in the future. You don't need to understand the Bible all at once, but the more you study, the more you'll learn and grow. Before your daily reading of the Word, ask God in prayer to show you how to apply what you're about to read. He will do just that. A good place to begin your Bible reading is in the Gospel of John. It's a profound, yet easy-to-understand book that vividly portrays the life and ministry of our Lord and Savior, Jesus Christ. The Gospel of John is the only book in the Bible that clearly states its purpose. The first chapter in the Book of John begins by declaring Christ as the living Word, "The Word became a man and lived among us" (***John 1:14***). Christ laid aside His deity and embraced His humanity so He would suffer as we suffer. He also sympathized with our weaknesses and helped us overcome temptations. What a Savior. The Book of John also declares Jesus as the Messiah. Consider the following scripture, "But these are written so that you can believe that Jesus is the Messiah, the Son of God. Then, by believing, you can have life through his name" (***John 20:31***).

John portrays the life and ministry of Jesus and demonstrates our Father's love for us in sending Himself to die for our sins. Many might die for a loved one, but who'll die for the guilty and undeserving? God did, through His son Jesus Christ.

God's love for us demonstrated on the cross should inspire you to believe in Jesus even more. Jesus is the Divine Light that came to dispel the spiritual darkness that engulfed the world. When we see Jesus as the Son of God, the Redeemer and Savior of the World, we come face to face with His glorious Light. When we accept Him into our hearts, we invite His Light to shine in and through us. Our purpose as witnesses in the world is not to attract people to us, but to draw people to Him and the Light that lives within us. Biblical truths that support this claim and help you share your faith with others include:

Christ Comes to the World

The Word became a man and lived among us. We saw his divine greatness—the greatness that belongs to the only Son of the Father. The Word was full of grace and truth (***John 1:14***). No one has ever seen God. The only Son is the one who has shown us what God is like. He is himself God and is very close to the Father (***John 1:18***).

Jesus and Nicodemus

I assure you, everyone must be born again. Anyone who is not born again cannot be in God's kingdom (***John 3:3***). The only life people get from their human parents is physical. But the new life that the Spirit gives a person is spiritual. Don't be surprised that I told you, 'You must be born again' (***John 3:6-7***). Yes, God loved the world so much that he gave his only Son, so that everyone who believes in him would not be lost but have eternal life. God sent his Son into the world. He did not send him to judge the world guilty, but to save the world through him (***John 3:16-17***).

The One Who Comes From Heaven

The Father loves the Son and has given him power over everything. Whoever believes in the Son has eternal life. But those who do not obey the Son will never have that life. They cannot get away from God's anger (***John 3:35-36***).

Jesus Talks to a Woman in Samaria

The woman answered, "I am surprised that you ask me for a drink! You are a Jew and I am a Samaritan woman!" (Jews have nothing to do with Samaritans). Jesus answered, "You don't know what God can give you. And you don't know who I am, the one who asked you for a drink. If you knew, you would have asked me, and I would have given you living water."

The woman said, "Sir, where will you get that living water? The well is very deep, and you have nothing to get water with. Are you greater than our ancestor Jacob? He is the one who gave us this well. He drank from it himself, and his sons and all his animals drank from it too." Jesus answered, "Everyone who drinks this water will be thirsty again. But anyone who drinks the water I give will never be thirsty again. The water I give people will be life a spring flowing inside them. It will bring them eternal life" (***John 4:9-14***).

Jesus, the Bread of Life

Everyone who sees the Son and believes in him has eternal life. I will raise them up on the last day. This is what my Father wants" (***John 6:40***).

It is the Spirit that gives life. The body is of no value for that. But the things I have told you are from the Spirit, so they give life (***John 6:63***).

The Jesus Leaders Against Jesus

If I don't do what my Father does, then don't believe what I say. But if I do what my Father does, you should believe in what I do. You might not believe in me, but you should believe in the things I do. Then you will know and understand that the Father is in me and I am in the Father (***John 10:37-38***).

Jesus Talks About Service

Whoever serves me must follow me. My servants must be with me everywhere I am. My Father will give honor to anyone who serves me (***John 12:26***).Jesus Talks About Love

I give you a new command: Love each other. You must love each other just as I loved you. All people will know that you are my followers if you love each other (***John 13:34-35***).

From Sinner to Salvation

Many people are offended when someone calls them a 'sinner,' and rightfully so, no one wants to be a wrongdoer against God. However, all mankind falls short of God's glory, and because we're all unrighteous, we're all sinners. So therefore, we all need salvation.

Salvation, however, is deliverance from the power and penalty of sin. This means you're no longer guilty of the sins committed against God; rather, your sins are made right through the blood of Jesus Christ. Your sins are washed in His blood and forgotten, every last one of them.

God delivers from the penalty of sin and brings you to a place of freedom, security and liberty in Him. This is the foundation of who you are in Christ and the platform from which to share your testimony. Not everyone will be so willing to hear about Christ, and at times, you may be ridiculed, rejected or even persecuted for your faith, but don't be discouraged. Christ, before His death on the cross, prayed you'd be his witness in the world, and in return, he promised to never leave you. So take courage, share the good news of the Gospel of Christ, and share your faith with others:

"I now belong to God the Father through His one and only unique son Jesus Christ." When mankind disobeyed God in the Garden of Eden, we became separated from God and punished with hard labor, physical pain, confusion, sickness, and death. God's Son Jesus is our only hope, belief and acceptance of him gives eternal life. Biblical truths that support this claim and help you share your faith with others include:

How God Makes People Right

God makes people right through their faith in Jesus Christ. He does this for all who believe in Christ. Everyone is the same. All have sinned and are not good enough to share God's divine greatness. They are made right with God by his grace. This is a free gift. They are right with God by being made free from sin through Jesus Christ (***Romans 3:22-24***).

Slaves of Goodness

But now you are free from sin. You have become slaves of God, and the result is that you live only for God. This will bring you eternal life. When people sin, they earn what sin pays—death. But God gives his people a free gift—eternal life in Christ Jesus our Lord (***Romans 6:22-23***).

Adam and Christ

Sin came into the world because of what one man did. And with sin came death. So this is why all people must die—because all people have sinned (***Romans 5:12***). So that one sin of Adam brought the punishment of death to all people. But in the same way, Christ did something so good that it makes all people right with God. And that brings them true life (***Romans 5:18***).

There is a way that people think is right, but it leads only to death (***Proverbs 14:12***).

"God loves everyone in the world and wants us all to know who He is." Our Father in Heaven provides peace and everlasting life. He sent His only son Jesus Christ to intercede on our behalf because He didn't want us to experience the pain and misery that life without Him brings. Jesus Christ was the best representation of Himself He could offer. He left nothing of Himself. He gave it all. Biblical truths that support this claim and help you share your faith with others include:

Right With God

We have been made right with God because of our faith. So we have peace with God through our Lord Jesus Christ. Through our faith, Christ has brought us into that blessing of God's grace that we now enjoy. And we are very happy because of the hope we have of sharing God's glory (***Romans 5:1-2***).

"Yes, God loved the world so much that he gave his only Son, so that everyone who believes in him would not be lost but have eternal life." The verse John 3:16 is the most important verse in the Bible. It tells us how much God loves us, why we're in need of His great love, and how to respond to that love. This self-sacrificial love is available to all who believe in Jesus Christ and are willing to call upon His name. Christ bridged the gap between man and God and brought us back into a relationship with our Father. If we remain faithful and obedient, we will one day live with God in eternity.

One Way to God

There is only one God, and there is only one way that people can reach God. That way is through Christ Jesus, who as a man gave himself to pay for everyone to be free. This is the message that was given to us at just the right time (***1 Timothy 2:5-6***).

Suffering for Doing Right

Christ himself suffered when he died for you, and with that one death he paid for your sins. He was not guilty, but he died for people who are guilty. He did this to bring all of you to God. In his physical form he was killed, but he was made alive by the Spirit (***1 Peter 3:18***).

Faith in God

But Christ died for us while we were still sinners, and by this God showed how much he loves us (***Romans 5:8***).

"God's ultimate act of love requires a response of faith in Him and His promises." The simple act of faith in a God that cannot be seen, touched or felt is the only response required by us. When we express unquestionable faith in Him and His Son, He offers His peace and shows us how to handle the brokenness we feel. God shows us how to rise above any situation and fly, even with broken wings, because the blood of Jesus restores and heals the brokenness in our lives.

What we did in the past no longer matters. No sin is too great and no pain too deep that the Father's love cannot touch and heal. Your confession of faith in Him not only saves you from sin, but also opens the door to an intimate relationship with God in Christ. Pray to God, share your heart with Him and He will share His heart with you. Biblical truths that support this claim and help you share your faith with others include:

Faith is what makes real the things we hope for. It is proof of what we cannot see (***Hebrews 11:1***).

Saved by Grace

I mean that you have been saved by grace because you believed. You did not save yourselves; it was a gift from God. You are not saved by the things you have done, so there is nothing to boast about. God has made us what we are. In Christ Jesus, God made us new people so that we would spend our lives doing the good things he had already planned for us to do (***Ephesians 2:8-10***).

Born Again

But some people did accept him. They believed in him, and he gave them the right to become children of God. They became God's children, but not in the way babies are usually born. It was not because of any human desire or plan. They were born from God himself (***John 1:12-13***).

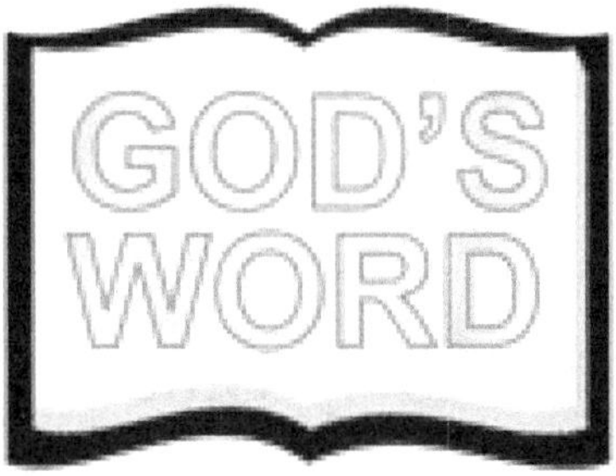

Part III – STUDY

"Let the word of Christ in all its richness
live in your hearts and make you wise"
(Colossians 3:16)

What is the Bible?

The Bible is the authoritative Word of God. No other book can make such a claim. Its authenticity may be questioned and authority denied, but its power to change the vilest of human beings into a saint can never be denied. Over the years, the Bible has withstood countless attacks. It's been banned, burned and outlawed; yet it still stands as the beacon of hope to a lost and dying world. It's the most recognized and most read book of all times and remains the world's best-selling book. Jesus Christ, the Word that became flesh, is God's revelation of Himself to us. He is the fulfillment of all hope and the Savior of the world. God's divine covenantal agreement to redeem mankind from sin and reconcile man to Himself is fulfilled in His life, death and resurrection. He fulfilled all the righteous requirements of the law written in the Old Testament. What we could not do for ourselves because of our disobedience, Christ accomplished through His obedience. The Word is God's only Word to man. It's like fire that cleanses (***Jeremiah 23:29***), a mirror that reveals (***James 1:23***), a lamp that illuminates (***Psalm 119:105***), and bread that satisfies (***Matthew 4:4***). Everything God desired to reveal to man is in the Bible. It has all that we need to grow in the grace of the Lord Jesus Christ. The Bible consists of the Old Testament and the New Testament.

The Old Testament was written in Hebrew and contains thirty-nine books in total:

- Five books of Law that trace God's dealing with mankind from the beginning through the time of the flood
- Twelve books of history that cover a period of one thousand years and pave the way for the coming Messiah, King and Redeemer
- Five books of poetry that unveil the realities of life and influences the sacred music used today in the worship of Jehovah
- Seventeen books of prophecy that reveal past, present and future events.
- The New Testament was written in Greek and contains twenty-seven books in total:
- Four books of the Gospel (Matthew, Mark, Luke, and John) presenting the life, death and resurrection of Jesus Christ, the

Messiah;

- One book of history (Acts) that offers a theological history of the expansion of the Christian church through the activity and work of the Holy Spirit in the lives of the apostles and early Christians;

- Twenty-one Pauline and Non-Pauline letters written in response to the situations Christians faced as they sought to preserve the account of the life, ministry, work, death, resurrection, and second coming of our Lord Jesus Christ; and

- One book of prophecy (Revelation) that reveals past, present and future events that will precede the second coming of Christ. Revelation applauds the victory of Christ and His people and shows the rewards that await those who will be faithful to the end. Before Christ's ascension to Heaven, He promised us He would leave us another comforter, the Holy Spirit, the Spirit of Grace and Truth, who would guide us into all truth and show us things to come.

This promise was fulfilled on the day of Pentecost, when 120 believers waited in unity for the promised Holy Spirit. The Holy Spirit endued the believers with His power and presence and they immediately became effective witnesses in the world. The Holy Spirit is the presence of God operating in the life of every believer and in the world. Although believers are filled with the Spirit and receive His seal at the time of conversion, they should seek His empowerment so they too will be an effective witness in the world.

Why is there an Old Testament and a New Testament?

The Old Testament is anchored in the covenants God made with His chosen people in Israel. The word covenant ('berith' in Hebrew) means to cut and testament ('diatheke' in Greek) means contract or agreement between two parties. The covenant or agreement God made with fallen man has infinite and divine origins, with the Holy Spirit, Jesus Christ, and the God-man acting as guarantors of the covenant. The Old Testament is two-dimensional as it studies the world's relationship to God and God's relationship to Israel.

The New Testament, on the other hand, examines the theology of the synoptic gospels: Acts, Paul, James, Peter, John, Hebrews, and the writers of the general epistles by analyzing the writings of each New Testament writer. The word 'gospel' is birthed from the Greek word that means 'good news.' The New Testament is the good news of Jesus written in a form of literature and is composed of four forms of literature: Gospels, Book of Acts, the Pauline and the Non-Pauline letters, and Revelation. Jesus' birth, work, death, resurrection, and return are the focal points of the New Testament. Jesus is the central figure in the New Testament and the radical fulfillment of the Old Testament.

Is the Bible just another religious book?

No, the Bible is a love letter from God with our personal address on it and a window through which we may look into eternity. The Word was inspired through the active agent of the Holy Spirit, the Third person of the Godhead, to over forty different authors between 1400 BC to AD 100. For one to accept the thirty-nine books of the Old Testament, 'the Covenant of Law,' and the twenty-seven books of the New Testament, 'the covenant of grace,' as being authoritative, one must accept the supreme authority and power of God. It is the DNA of divine infallible truth. In authority, it's the gavel of man's conscience and the verdict of one's life. It's by the Word that all things were created, seen and unseen, and it's by the Word that all things are upheld.

What are the Ten Commandments?

Rules, rules, rules! No one likes rules. Rules seem to limit our freedom, sentencing us to a life of boredom. But in reality, we can't live without them. Rules exist to maintain order in our society and control behavior of those who would otherwise act unruly. God also has rules, but they're different. His rules are to guide his children into having a meaningful and intimate relationship with Him. God's rules tell us what pleases and displeases Him.

They're called the Ten Commandments. God gave them to Moses over 3,000 years ago to show the nation of Israel, who worshipped the pagan gods while they were in bondage in Egypt, how to, after they had been delivered, live in this new relationship with Him. Our deliverance from sin also marked a pivotal point in our lives. Before we met Christ, we were serving and worshipping the gods of this world. So it should come as no surprise that God gives us rules for our new relationship with Him. He took the Ten Commandments He gave to the children of Israel and gave us only one commandment that encompasses them all, "I give you a new command: Love each other. You must love each other just as I loved you. All people will know that you are my followers if you love each other" **(John 13:34-35).**

In doing this one commandment, we fulfill the ten. Let us love one another.

The Ten Commandments:

1.You shall have no other gods before me.

2.You shall not make for yourself any carved image, or any likeness of anything that is in heaven above, or that is in the earth beneath, or that is in the water under the earth; you shall not bow down to them nor serve them. For I, the Lord your God, am a jealous God, visiting the iniquity of the fathers on the children to the third and fourth generations of those who hate me, but showing mercy to thousands, to those who love Me and keep My commandments.

3.You shall not take the name of the Lord your God in vain, for the Lord will not hold him guiltless who takes His name in vain.

4.Remember the Sabbath day, to keep it holy. Six days you shall labor and do all your work, but the seventh day is the Sabbath of the Lord your God. In it you shall do no work: you, nor your son, nor your daughter, nor your manservant, nor your maidservant, nor your cattle, nor your stranger who is within your gates. For in six days the Lord made the heavens and the earth, the sea, and all that is in them, and rested the seventh day. Therefore the Lord blessed the Sabbath day and hallowed it.

5.Honor your father and your mother, that your days may be long upon the land which the Lord your God is giving you.

6.You shall not murder.

7.You shall not commit adultery.

8.You shall not steal.

9.You shall not bear false witness against your neighbor.

10.You shall not covet your neighbor's house; you shall not covet your neighbor's wife, nor his manservant, nor his maidservant, nor his ox, nor his donkey, nor anything that is your neighbor's."

How do I study the Bible?

Before you begin your daily study of the Word, you must seek the guidance of the Holy Spirit through prayer. Prayer is the first step to purposeful Bible study. Pray for guidance on what to study and listen carefully, sometimes there's a message God wants you to hear and will guide you to a specific verse of chapter in the Bible. Also pray for the appropriate interpretation and application of the Word of God in your life. Then, decide on a method of study. I recommend the 3R's: Read, Record, and Respond. This process requires you to read the word, record your thoughts and respond to what you learn.

Step 1: READ

Choose a verse or chapter based on your prayer, then skim the entire book to get a panoramic view of the author's message. It's like standing on top of a mountain and enjoying the sheer beauty of the entire landscape, the key here is to focus on the big picture.

As you skim, pay attention to the chapter headings and titles and paraphrase them in your own words. This helps you remember what you read. Have fun with the process, God knows your intention is not to change His Word, but to understand it, so be creative.

Then, identify the Biblical author and the historical setting. By understanding the circumstances in which the author wrote the message, the meaning of the text will become clearer to you. You may even find yourself exclaiming, "So this is why he wrote this passage!" This process strengthens your interpretation of the Word of God.

At this point, remind yourself to not subject the text to your preconceived ideas. Allow your mind and spirit to be submitted to and influenced by the mind of the Biblical author, the Divine author, and the text itself. After all, this is God's inspired Word to you, so you must be inspired as well. Allow God to speak to you as you read. Also, always distinguish when God or Jesus speaks and whom they address. Some Bibles print Jesus' words in red ink to help in this process.

If you come across a difficult passage, don't give up. Go to God in prayer and ask for help. Ask Him to remove all distractions, such as anxiety, noise and judgments that interfere with His message. If you're patient as you pray, God will help you regain your focus. As you continue reading, you may find yourself with more questions than answers. God welcomes your questions because He knows you seek Him. He will use the very questions you have to point you in the right direction, and in time the answers will be revealed.

Step 2: RECORD

Record in this sense means to write. Writing is very important as you study and interact with God's Word. Record your comments, questions, passing thoughts, and impressions in one place, perhaps a notebook or word document. This makes it easier to refer to your notes at a later date. If you record as you study, then you'll be able to continue from where you left off without having to go back to the beginning.

Furthermore, when you write down what you learn, you stand a greater chance of retaining the information. Writing also has a way of opening up the mind and propelling you into deeper levels of understanding. All that has been given to us in the Word of God came as a result of someone writing it down. So record your thoughts, God may use your words to touch another person's life. You never know.

Step 3: RESPOND

The third and final step is to respond, or apply, what you learn. As you study the Word of God, you'll notice the various areas in your life that need to change. There might be some thoughts, habits, behaviors, and attitudes that need to be corrected or improved. There are also spiritual disciplines, like prayer, fasting, meditation, worship, fellowship, serving, evangelism, and stewardship that need to be practiced.

Whatever it is, just know that any change toward God in your life, no matter how small it seems, is well worth it. In time, you'll experience spiritual growth and maturity in areas you were never aware of. With time, you'll find many truths that our loving Father has jeweled in His Word to enable you to live a victorious Christian life.

What should I look for in the Bible?

First, pay attention to similarities and differences in the Bible. There are countless examples that are meant to be noticed. Read carefully and find out what truths God desires you to learn from those things that are alike. There's also a lot to learn from observing and comparing differences. Differences are sometimes subtle and easy to miss. Read carefully and take notice. One example is the size difference between David and Goliath. It shows us how God uses the small and seemingly weak to accomplish great things. He places extraordinary people in ordinary packages to succeed in impossible situations so He can show forth His might and power. Second, notice repetition, it's one of God's ways of raising His voice and getting our attention. "Enough already, I get the picture!" is a typical response from someone who's annoyed at hearing the same thing over and over again. Words and actions that are repeated over time generally become who you are. We are what we speak right? Or better yet, we are what we repeat. Repetitions are there for a reason, so read carefully and God will show you what He desires you to learn.

Next, apply historical illustrations to modern time. Although many of the settings and circumstances illustrated in the Bible are not common to the present-day reader, the principles can be applied to today's setting. For example, in Mark 4:30-33, a 'mustard seed' is used to illustrate God's kingdom:

Then Jesus said, "What can I use to show you what God's kingdom is like? What story can I use to explain it? God's kingdom is like a mustard seed, which is smaller than any other seed on earth that you can plant. But when you plant it, it grows and becomes the largest of all the plants in your garden. It has branches that are very big. The wild birds can come and make nests there and be protected from the sun." Jesus used many stories like these to teach the people. He taught them all they could understand.

The author's intention shows us size does not matter to God. He can take something as small as a mustard seed and make it into something larger than life. With faith, God will make something great out of your life too. Also take note of name changes. God changed the name of several individuals when He revealed His plan and purpose for their lives. The name Jacob, for instance, means "he who supplants." Jacob's name was later changed to Israel, meaning "God prevails" after he stole his brother's blessing, ran away in fear, and fought with God for the blessing. It was after his name was changed that he received a new identity. Another notable name change is Saul of Tarsus, a persecutor of the church, who had his name changed to Paul the Apostle after he received a revelation of the risen Christ. He was given his commission by God to be an apostle to the Gentiles. In the end, these men were faithful to God.

If we remain faithful, you too will receive a new name, "Everyone who hears this should listen to what the Spirit says to the churches! I will give the hidden manna to everyone who wins the victory. I will also give each one a white stone that has a new name written on it. And no one will know this name expect the one who gets the stone" (***Revelation 2:17***). So what's in a name? A whole lot so pay close attention to those name changes. Take note of the capitalization of words as well, such as Spirit and spirit. The uppercase 'S' in the word Spirit denotes power and authority and always refers to God's Spirit and the Holy Spirit. On the other hand, the lower-case 's' in the word spirit refers to any spirit other than God. A careful reading of the Word will highlight these subtle nuances and help you avoid incorrect interpretation and application of the Word. Lastly, use the resources available to you to seek God. The internet, for instance, can be a helpful tool to strengthen your faith. Some websites to help you learn more about God include:

http://www.focusonthefamily.org
http://www.bible.com
http://www.biblegateway.com
http://www.700club.com

What do I need for Bible study?

First, you need a Bible. There are a variety of Bibles available on the market today and it can be quite daunting to choose one. The King James Bible or the Amplified Bible is a good first Bible, as well as a teen or children's Bible for easier-to-understand versions. I also recommend downloading a Bible application to your phone or computer from www.biblegateway.com. Thc wcbsite provides Bible text in nearly every version and almost any language, as well as audio Bibles in various formats, all free of cost.

Secondly, consider investing in a Bible Concordance. This book is a verbal index of the Bible, which lists Biblical words and their explanations alphabetically, and is often found in several translations. A complete yet simple Bible concordance will help you locate any verse in the Bible with an explanation of its contents. I recommend the Young's Analytical Concordance or the Gruden's Complete Concordance.

Lastly, consider a Bible Dictionary because what a word means today is far from what it meant centuries ago. An incorrect meaning of a word or misunderstanding of a Biblical text may result in the incorrect application. A Bible Dictionary also provides the history and meaning of a word, the context in which it's being used, and ultimately the author's intentions. I recommend Vine's Expository Dictionary of the Old & New Testament Words or the New Unger's Bible Dictionary.

Should I memorize Bible verses?

Yes, we should all memorize verses in the Bible. Having a few verses memorized comes in handy. Why? You never know when and where you'll need a verse to fight against sin, solve a problem, or encourage another person. Memorizing takes time, but it can be easy and fun. To memorize a verse, read it aloud over and over until it becomes familiar. Then, write the verses several times while creating a picture in your mind. This exercise will help you memorize any verse you choose. You may also ask a friend or family member to read the verse back to you. And if you're still having difficulty remembering, write the verse in bold letters on several pieces of paper and post them on your bedroom wall, bathroom mirror, refrigerator door, closet door, computer monitor, or put them anywhere you'll see and read it daily. After a while, you'll remember those verses. Try and commit to learning a few

Bible verses each month. You'll be surprised at how much you can remember. Ask God to help you as well, He wants you to know His word.

Why did Jesus use parables (short stories)?

A short story is one of the best ways to make what you're saying more interesting, captivating, and memorable. We almost always remember a good story. Jesus knew this so He used short simple stories, called parables, to get the attention of His audience and to get His point across. You should familiarize yourself with the parables of Jesus. They can be found in the gospels of Matthew, Mark, Luke, and John in the New Testament. One thing you'll notice is Jesus used simple life illustrations familiar to His audience. You can do the same to share your faith. Find those short interesting stories people around you can identify with and use them to start a conversation. Never embellish the story to make it sound better. God doesn't need you to make His story better; the truth is always a great story.

What do these words mean?

Here is a list of words as a believer you'll need to become familiar with. You'll find them showing up often in your conversation and life.

Atonement: to make amends; compensate for loss

Blame: to find fault with someone other than yourself for something you could have been the cause of

Conversion: to actually change

Deception: to deny something you know to be true

Doctrine: a belief that is taught

Faith: belief and trust with allegiance and confidence; to rely on and trust in

Feelings: a fluctuating emotion that cannot be completely trusted and must be supported by facts to be true

Lie: something you can change when you want; anything not 100% truth

Meditation: contemplate; focus on

Motive: the real reason you do something; something only you and God know

Opinion: what you believe without properly having all the facts

Practice: to perform repeatedly; to become proficient through repetition

Prayer: an earnest request; the addressing of divinity; dialogue between God and His people

Process: series of actions directed toward a result

Repentance: to turn away from

Salvation: saving someone from sin

Satan: devil; supreme spirit of evil; number one enemy of everything God loves

Sin: rebellion against God; the root cause of all humanity's problems; always an offense against God

Temptation:	something that tempts; person, place or thing
Time:	the most valuable commodity in life; something God has an unlimited amount of and we don't
Truth:	something you cannot change
Worldly:	devoted to this world and its pursuits

How can the Bible help me?

Because God cares about you and your wellbeing, His Word provides solutions to your problems. The Word of God is the best remedy for your problem and will help you grow in the grace and love of Christ. There's healing and restoration in the blood of Jesus, therefore, healing and deliverance is prescribed in the Word of God. Just as you should go to the doctor's office when you're physically ill, you should go to the Word of God to feel better as well. Below are God's promises for your healing:

I feel down and low: Give all your worries to him, because he cares for you (***1 Peter 5:7***).

I feel alone: I am with you, and I will protect you everywhere you go. I will bring you back to this land. I will not leave you until I have done what I have promised (***Genesis 28:15***).

My heart's broken: The Lord is close to those who have suffered disappointment. He saves those who are discouraged (***Psalm 34:18***).

I'm worried: Don't worry about anything, but pray and ask God for everything you need, always giving thanks for what you have (***Philippians 4:6***).

I'm afraid: The Spirit God gave us does not make us afraid. His Spirit is a source of power and love and self-control (***2 Timothy 1:7***)

I'm angry: When you are angry, don't let that anger make you sin, and don't stay angry all day. Don't give the devil a way to defeat you (***Ephesians 4:26-27***). Anger is cruel and can destroy like a flood, but jealousy is much worse (Proverbs 27:4).

I'm jealous: A fool's anger will kill him. His jealousy will destroy him (***Job 5:2***). Peace of mind makes the body healthy, but jealousy is like a cancer (***Proverbs 14:30***).

I'm lost: If you wander from the right path, either to the right or to the left, you will hear a voice behind you saying, "You should go this way. Here is the right way (***Isaiah 30:21***).

I'm sick: And I will bring your health back and heal your wounds, says the Lord, because other people said you were outcasts. They said, 'No one cares about Zion' (***Jeremiah 30:17***).

I'm sad: He will wipe away every tear from their eyes. There will be no more death, sadness, crying, or pain. All the old ways are gone (***Revelation 21:4***).

I'm confused: God is not a God of confusion but a God of peace. This is the rule for all the meetings of God's people (***1 Corinthians 14:33***).

I'm ashamed: But if we confess our sins, God will forgive us. We can trust God to do this. He always does what is right. He will make us clean from all the wrong things we have done (***1 John 1:9***).

I'm guilty: I assure you, anyone who hears what I say and believes in the one who sent me has eternal life. They will not be judged guilty. They have already left death and have entered into life (***John 5:24***).

I feel like a failure: The Lord lifts up people who have fallen. He helps those who are in trouble (***Psalm 145:14***).

I'm losing faith: Faith is what makes real the things we hope for. It is proof of what we cannot see (***Hebrews 11:1***).

I'm losing hope: I say this because I know the plans that I have for you. This message is from the Lord. I have good plans for you. I don't plan to hurt you. I plan to give you hope and a good future (***Jeremiah 29:11***).

I'm doubtful: If you stand before others and are willing to say you believe in me, then I will tell my Father in heaven that you belong to me. But if you stand before others and say you do not believe in me, then I will tell my Father in heaven that you do not belong to me (***Matthew10:32-33***).

I'm indecisive: Say only 'yes' if you mean 'yes,' and say only 'no' if you mean 'no.' If you say more than that, it is from the Evil One (***Matthew 5:37***).

I'm unworthy: God never changes his mind about the people he calls. He never decides to take back the blessings he has given them (***Romans 11:29***).

I'm lost: The person who is right with me will live by trusting in me. But I will not be pleased with the one who turns back in fear. But we are not those who turn back and are lost. No, we are the people who have faith and are saved (***Hebrews 10:38-39***).

I'm impatient: You must be patient. After you have done what God wants, you will get what he promised you (***Hebrews 10:36***).

I have lustful eyes: Keep your eyes on the path, and look straight ahead (***Proverbs 4:25***).

I'm frustrated with my children: Children do foolish things, but if you punish them, they will learn not to do them (***Proverbs 22:15***).

I'm frustrated with my parents: Wise children make their parents happy. Foolish children bring them shame (***Proverbs 15:20***).

I want to be rich: It is better to be respected than to be rich. A good name is worth more than silver or gold. The rich and the poor are the same. The Lord made them all (***Proverbs 22:1-2***).

I don't want to be poor: These two things will make you poor: hurting the poor to make yourself rich and giving gifts to the rich (***Proverbs 22:16***).

I'm unfaithful: The sin of adultery is a trap, and the Lord gets very angry with those who fall into it (Proverbs 22:14).

I have enemies: I'm telling you to love your enemies and do good to them. Lend to people without expecting to get anything back. If you do this, you will have a great reward. You will be children of the Most High God. Yes, because God is good even to the people who are full of sin and not thankful (***Luke 6:35***).

Part IV – DISCERN

"But keep the Lord Christ holy in your hearts. Always be ready to answer everyone who asks you to explain about the hope you have in Jesus Christ"
(1 Peter 3:15)

Who, What and Why?

Many believers will confess an embarrassing moment when they didn't know the answer to a question about their faith. This happens. The truth is we'll never know all the answers about God. Be patient with yourself, you're not expected to have all the answers. But, you should know who God is, what you believe, and why you believe what you believe so you can confidently and adequately defend your faith. Always be ready to give a Biblical response to questions about your faith, but do it courteously and respectfully.

This section is designed to help minimize those on-the-spot

embarrassing moments by providing Biblical answers in a simple and straightforward manner and to initiate meaningful conversations with believers and non-believers alike as well. The responses are quoted directly from the Easy-to-Read version of the Bible.

But before you read any further, you must know this: faith is the foundation of who you are in the Lord. Without faith, you won't accomplish anything for God. To please God, you must believe in Him and the Word. And since Jesus is the Word that became flesh, and Jesus and God are one and the same, then to please God, you must believe in His Son Jesus as well. Now, let's get some questions answered.

Who is God?

God is spirit. So the people who worship him must worship in spirit and truth (***John 4:24***). Anyone who says, "I believe that Jesus is the Son of God," is a person who lives in God, and God lives in that person. So we know the love that God has for us, and we trust that love. God is love. Everyone who lives in love lives in God, and God lives in them (***1 John 4:15-16***). Jesus answered, "I am the way, the truth, and the life. The only way to the Father is through me. If you really knew me, you would know my Father too. But now you know the Father. You have seen him." Philip said to him, "Lord, show us the Father. That is all we need." Jesus answered, "Philip, I have been with you for a long time. So you should know me. Anyone who has seen me has seen the Father too. So why do you say, 'Show us the Father'? Don't you believe that I am in the Father and the Father is in me? The things I have told you don't come from me. The Father lives in me, and he is doing his own work. Believe me when I say that I am in the Father and the Father is in me. Or believe because of the miracles I have done (***John 14:6-11***).

Who is Jesus?

No one can see God, but the Son is exactly like God. He rules over everything that has been made. Through his power all things were made: things in heaven and on earth, seen and not seen—all spiritual rulers, lords, powers, and authorities. Everything was made through him and for him. The Son was there before anything was made. And all things continue because of him. He is the head of the body, which is the church. He is the beginning of everything else. And he is the first among all who will be raised from death. So in everything he is most important. God was pleased for all of himself to live in the Son. And through him, God was happy to bring all things back to himself again—things on earth and things in heaven. God made peace by using the blood sacrifice of his Son on the cross (***Colossians 1:15-20***).

Who is the Holy Spirit?

But the fruit of the Spirit is love, joy, peace, forbearance, kindness, goodness, faithfulness, gentleness and self-control.

Against such things there is no law (***Galatians 5:22-23***). So now anyone who is in Christ Jesus is not judged guilty. That is because in Christ Jesus the law of the Spirit that brings life made you free. It made you free from the law that brings sin and death.

The law was without power because it was made weak by our sinful selves. But God did what the law could not do: He sent his own Son to earth with the same human life that everyone else uses for sin. God sent him to be an offering to pay for sin. So God used a human life to destroy sin. He did this so that we could be right just as the law said we must be. Now we don't live following our sinful selves. We live following the Spirit. People who live following their sinful selves think only about what they want. But those who live following the Spirit are thinking about what the Spirit wants them to do. If your thinking is controlled by your sinful self, there is spiritual death. But if your thinking is controlled by the Spirit, there is life and peace. Why is this true? Because anyone whose thinking is controlled by their sinful self is against God.

They refuse to obey God's law. And really they are not able to obey it. Those who are ruled by their sinful selves cannot please God. But you are not ruled by your sinful selves. You are ruled by the Spirit, if that Spirit of God really lives in you. But whoever does not have the Spirit of Christ does not belong to Christ. Your body will always be dead because of sin. But if Christ is in you, then the Spirit gives you life, because Christ made you right with God. God raised Jesus from death. And if God's Spirit lives in you, he will also give life to your bodies that die. Yes, God is the one who raised Christ from death, and he will raise you to life through his Spirit living in you. So, my brothers and sisters, we must not be ruled by our sinful selves.

We must not live the way our sinful selves want. If you use your lives to do what your sinful selves want, you will die spiritually. But if you use the Spirit's help to stop doing the wrong things you do with your body, you will have true life. The true children of God are those who let God's Spirit lead them (R***omans 8:1-14***). Also, the Spirit helps us. We are very weak, but the Spirit helps us with our weakness. We don't know how to pray as we should, but the Spirit himself speaks to God for us. He begs God for us, speaking to him with feelings too deep for words. God already knows our deepest thoughts. And he understands what the Spirit is saying, because the Spirit speaks for his people in the way that agrees with what God wants (***Romans 8:26-30***).

So I tell you, live the way the Spirit leads you. Then you will not do the evil things your sinful self wants. The sinful self wants what is against the Spirit, and the Spirit wants what is against the sinful self. They are always fighting against each other, so that you don't do what you really want to do (***Galatians 5:16-17***). Great blessings belong to those who want to do right more than anything else. God will fully satisfy them (***Matthew 5:6***).

So I beg you, brothers and sisters, because of the great mercy God has shown us, offer your lives as a living sacrifice to him—an offering that is only for God and pleasing to him. Considering what he has done, it is only right that you should worship him in this way. Don't change yourselves to be like the people of this world, but let God change you inside with a new way of thinking. Then you will be able to understand and accept what God wants for you. You will be able to know what is good and pleasing to him and what is perfect (***Romans 12:1-2***).

Without faith no one can please God. Whoever comes to God

must believe that he is real and that he rewards those who sincerely try to find him (***Hebrews 11:6***).

Why seek God?

God wanted people to look for him, and perhaps in searching all around for him, they would find him. But he is not far from any of us. It is through him that we are able to live, to do what we do, and to be who we are. As your own poets have said, 'We all come from him.' That's right. We all come from God. So you must not think that he is like something people imagine or make. He is not made of gold, silver, or stone. In the past people did not understand God, and he overlooked this. But now he is telling everyone in the world to change and turn to him. He has decided on a day when he will judge all the people in the world in a way that is fair. To do this he will use a man he chose long ago. And he has proved to everyone that this is the man to do it. He proved it by raising him from death! (***Acts 17:27-31***).

Why obey God?

If we obey what God has told us to do, then we are sure that we know him. If we say we know God but do not obey his commands, we are lying. The truth is not in us. But when we obey God's teaching, his love is truly working in us. This is how we know that we are living in him. If we say we live in God, we must live the way Jesus lived (***1 John 2:3-6***).

What is heaven?

Jesus said, "Don't be troubled. Trust in God, and trust in me. There are many rooms in my Father's house. I would not tell you this if it were not true. I am going there to prepare a place for you. After I go and prepare a place for you, I will come back. Then I will take you with me, so that you can be where I am. You know the way to the place where I am going" (***John 14:1-4***). The angel showed me the river of the water of life, clear as crystal. The river flows from the throne of God and the Lamb. It flows down the middle of the street of the city. The tree of life is one each side of the river, and it produces fruit every month, twelve times a year. The leaves of the tree are for healing the nations. Nothing that God judges guilty will be there in that city. The throne of God and the Lamb will be in the city. God's servants will worship him. They will see his face. God's name will be written on their foreheads.

There will never be night again. People will not need the light of a lamp or the light of the sun. The Lord God will give them light. And they will rule like kings forever and ever (***Revelation 22:1-5***). Once again, the kingdom of heaven is like a net that was let down into the lake and caught all kinds of fish. When it was full, the fishermen pulled it up on the shore. Then they sat down and collected the good fish in baskets, but threw the bad away. This is how it will be at the end of the age. The angels will come and separate the wicked from the righteous and throw them into the blazing furnace, where there will be weeping and gnashing of teeth (***Matthew 13:47-50***). Nothing unclean will ever enter the city. No one who does shameful things or tells lies will ever enter the city. Only those whose names are written in the Lamb's book of life will enter the city (***Revelation 21:27***).

What is true forgiveness?

Then Peter came to Jesus and asked, "Lord, when someone won't stop doing wrong to me, how many times must I forgive? Seven times?" Jesus answered, "I tell you, you must forgive them more than seven times. You must continue to forgive them even if they do wrong to you seventy times seven" (***Matthew 18:21-22***). This king did the same as my heavenly Father will do to you. You must forgive your brother or sister with all your heart, or my heavenly Father will not forgive you (***Matthew 18:21-35***). And when you stand praying, if you hold anything against anyone, forgive them, so that your Father in heaven may forgive you your sins (***Mark 11:25-26***). But I tell you, love your enemies. Pray for those who treat you badly. If you do this, you will be children who are truly like your Father in heaven. He lets the sun rise for all people, whether they are good or bad. He sends rain to those who do right and to those who do wrong. If you love only those who love you, why should you get a reward for that? Even the tax collectors do that. And if you are nice only to your friends, you are no better than anyone else. Even the people who don't know God are nice to their friends. What I am saying is that you must be perfect, just as your Father in heaven is perfect (***Matthew 5:44-48***).

What is discernment?

My dear friends, many false prophets are in the world now. So don't believe every spirit, but test the spirits to see if they are from God. This is how you can recognize God's Spirit. One spirit says, "I believe that Jesus is the Messiah who came to earth and became a man." That Spirit is from God. Another spirit refuses to say this about Jesus. That spirit is not from God. This is the spirit of the enemy of Christ. You have heard that the enemy of Christ is coming, and now he is already in the world (***1 John 4:1-3***).

Why study the Bible?

All Scripture is given by God. And all Scripture is useful for teaching and for showing people what is wrong in their lives. It is useful for correcting faults and teaching the right way to live. Using the Scriptures, those who serve God will be prepared and will have everything they need to do every good work (***2 Timothy 3:16-17***). Great blessings belong to those who don't listen to evil advice, who don't live like sinners, and who don't join those who make fun of God. Instead, they love the Lord's teachings and think about them day and night. So they grow strong, like a tree planted by a stream—a tree that produces fruit when it should and has leaves that never fall. Everything they do is successful (***Psalm 1:1-3***).

What is prayer?

When you pray, don't be like the hypocrites. They love to stand in the synagogues and on the street corners and pray loudly. They want people to see them. The truth is, that's all the reward they will get. But when you pray, you should go into your room and close the door. Then pray to your Father. He is there in that private place. He can see what is done in private, and he will reward you. And when you pray, don't be like the people who don't know God. They say the same things again and again. They think that if they say it enough, their god will hear them. Don't be like them. Your Father knows what you need before you ask him. So this is how you should pray: 'Our Father in heaven, we pray that your name will always be kept holy. We pray that your kingdom will come—that what you want will be done here on earth, the same as in heaven. Give us the food we need for today. Forgive our sins, just as we have forgiven those who did wrong to us. Don't let us be tempted, but save us from the Evil One.' Yes, if you forgive others for the wrongs they do to you, then your Father in heaven will also forgive your wrongs. But if you don't forgive others, then your Father in heaven will not forgive the wrongs you do (***Matthew 6:5-15***). Don't worry about anything, but pray and ask God for everything you need, always giving thanks for what you have (***Philippians 4:6***).

Why share the good news?

What good people produce is like a life-giving tree. Those who are wise give new life to others. If good people are rewarded here on earth, then surely those who do evil will also get what they deserve (***Proverbs 11:30-31***). But keep the Lord Christ holy in your hearts. Always be ready to answer everyone who asks you to explain about the hope you have (***1 Peter 3:15***).

How do I live according to God?

If you come to me but will not leave your family, you cannot by my follower. You must love me more than your father, mother, wife, children, brothers, and sisters—even more than your own life! Whoever will not carry the cross that is given to them when they follow me cannot be my follower (***Luke 14:26-27***). Then Jesus noticed that some of the guests were choosing the best places to sit. So he told this story: "When someone invites you to a wedding, don't sit in the most important seat. They may have invited someone more important than you. And if you are sitting in the most important seat, they will come to you and say, 'Give this man your seat!' Then you will have to move down to the last place and be embarrassed. So when someone invites you, go sit in the seat that is not important. Then they will come to you and say, 'Friend, move up here to this better place!' What an honor this will be for you in front of all the other guests. Everyone who makes themselves important will be made humble. But everyone who makes themselves humble will be made important" (***Luke 14:7-14***). Then he said to them all: "Whoever wants to be my disciple must deny themselves and take up their cross daily and follow me. For whoever wants to save their life will lose it, but whoever loses their life for me will save it. What good is it for someone to gain the whole world, and yet lose or forfeit their very self? (***Luke 9:23-25***).

What is hell?

Jesus said, "There was a rich man who always dressed in the finest clothes. He was so rich that he was able to enjoy all the best things every day. There was also a very poor man named Lazarus. Lazarus' body was covered with sores. He was often put by the rich man's gate. Lazarus wanted only to eat the scraps of food left on the floor under the rich man's table. And the dogs came and licked his sores. Later, Lazarus died. The angels took him and placed him in the arms of Abraham. The rich man also died and was buried. He was sent to the place of death and was in great pain. He saw Abraham far away with Lazarus in his arms. He called, 'Father Abraham, have mercy on me! Send Lazarus to me so that he can dip his finger in water and cool my tongue. I am suffering in this fire!' But Abraham said, 'My child, remember when you lived? You had all the good things in life. But Lazarus had nothing but problems. Now he is comforted here, and you are suffering. Also, there is a big pit between you and us. No one can cross over to help you, and no one can come here from there.' The rich man said, 'Then please, father Abraham, send Lazarus to my father's house on earth. I have five brothers. He could warn my brothers so that they will not come to this place of pain.' But Abraham said, 'They have the Law of Moses and the writings of the prophets to read; let them learn from that.' The rich man said, 'No, father Abraham! But if someone came to them from the dead, then they would decide to change their lives.' But Abraham said to him, 'If your brothers won't listen to Moses and the prophets, they won't listen to someone who comes back from the dead" (***Luke 16:19-31***).

Who is the enemy?

Son of man, sing this sad song about the king of Tyre. Say to him, "This is what the Lord God says: You were the perfect man—so full of wisdom and perfectly handsome. You were in Eden, the garden of God. You had every precious stone—rubies, topaz, and diamonds, beryls, onyx, and jasper, sapphires, turquoise, and emeralds. And each of these stones was set in gold. You were given this beauty on the day you were created. God made you strong. You were one of the chosen Cherubs who spread your wings over my throne. I put you on the holy mountain of God. You walked among the jewels that sparkled like fire. You were good and honest when I created you, but then you became evil. Your business brought you many riches. But they also put cruelty inside you, and you sinned. So I treated you like something unclean and threw you off the mountain of God. You were one of the chosen Cherubs who spread your wings over my throne. But I forced you to leave the jewels that sparkled like fire. Your beauty made you proud. Your glory ruined your wisdom. So I threw you down to the ground, and now other kings stare at you. You did many wrong things. You were a very crooked merchant. In this way you made the holy places unclean. So I brought fire from inside you. It burned you! You burned to ashes on the ground. Now everyone can see your shame. All the people in other nations were shocked about what happened to you. What happened to you will make people very afraid. You are finished!" (***Ezekiel 28:12-19***).

So be humble under God's powerful hand. Then he will lift you up when the right time comes. Give all your worries to him, because he cares for you. Control yourselves and be careful! The devil is your enemy, and he goes around like a roaring lion looking for someone to attack and eat. Refuse to follow the devil. Stand strong in your faith. You know that your brothers and sisters all over the world are having the same sufferings that you have. Yes, you will suffer for a short time. But after that, God will make everything right. He will make you strong. He will support you and keep you from falling. He is the God who gives all grace. He chose you to share in his glory in Christ. That glory will continue forever. All power is his forever. Amen (***1 Peter 5:6-11***).

Do you know where your fights and arguments come from? They come from the selfish desires that make war inside you. You want things, but you don't get them. So you kill and are jealous of others. But you still cannot get what you want. So you argue and fight. You don't get what you want because you don't ask God. Or when you ask, you don't receive anything, because the reason you ask is wrong. You only want to use it for your own pleasure. You people are not faithful to God! You should know that loving what the world has is the same as hating God. So anyone who wants to be friends with this evil world becomes God's enemy. Do you think the Scriptures mean nothing?

The Scriptures say, "The Spirit God made to live in us wants us only for himself." But the kindness God shows is greater. As the Scripture says, "God is against the proud, but he is kind to the humble. So give yourselves to God. Stand against the devil, and he will run away from you. Come near to God and he will come near to you. You are sinners, so clean sin out of your lives. You are trying to follow God and the world at the same time. Make your thinking pure. Be sad, be sorry, and cry! Change your laughter into crying. Change your joy into sadness. Be humble before the Lord, and he will make you great (***James 4:1-10***)

What are the enemy's abilities?

The Good News that we tell people may be hidden, but it is hidden only to those who are lost. The ruler of this world has blinded the minds of those who don't believe. They cannot see the light of the Good News—the message about the divine greatness of Christ. Christ is the one who is exactly like God (***2 Corinthians 4:3-4***).

What are the enemy's limitations?

The Lord will rescue me from every evil attack and will bring me safely to his heavenly kingdom. To him be glory for ever and ever. Amen (***2 Timothy 4:18***).

What is marriage?

Be willing to serve each other out of respect for Christ. Wives, be willing to serve your husbands the same as the Lord. A husband is the head of his wife, just as Christ is the head of the church. Christ is the Savior of the church, which is his body. The church serves under Christ, so it is the same with you wives. You should be willing to serve your husbands in everything. Husbands, love your wives the same as Christ loved the church and gave his life for it. He died to make the church holy. He used the telling of the Good News to make the church clean by washing it with water. Christ died so that he could give the church to himself like a bride in all her beauty. He died so that the church could be holy and without fault, with no evil or sin or any other thing wrong in it. And husbands should love their wives like that. They should love their wives as they love their own bodies. The man who loves his wife loves himself, because no one ever hates his own body, but feeds and takes care of it. And that is what Christ does for the church because we are parts of his body.

The Scriptures say, "That is why a man will leave his father and mother and join his wife, and the two people will become one" (***Ephesians 5:21-31***).

Now I will discuss the things you wrote me about. You asked if it is better for a man not to have any sexual relations at all. But sexual sin is a danger, so each man should enjoy his own wife, and each woman should enjoy her own husband. The husband should give his wife what she deserves as his wife. And the wife should give her husband what he deserves as her husband. The wife does not have power over her own body. Her husband has the power over her body. And the husband does not have power over his own body. His wife has the power over his body. Don't refuse to give your bodies to each other. But you might both agree to stay away from sex for a while so that you can give your time to prayer. Then come together again so that Satan will not be able to tempt you in your weakness.

I say this only to give you permission to be separated for a time. It is not a rule (***1 Corinthians 7:1-6***). If you find a wife, you have found something good. She shows that the Lord is happy with you (***Proverbs 18:22***). Now about sex and marriage: Drink only the water that comes from your own well, and don't let your water flow out into the streets. Keep it for yourself, and don't share it with strangers. Be happy with your own wife. Enjoy the woman you married while you were young. She is like a beautiful deer, a lovely fawn. Let her love satisfy you completely. Stay drunk on her love, and don't go stumbling into the arms of another woman. The Lord clearly sees everything you do. He watches where you go (***Proverbs 5:15-21***).

What is divorce?

Some Pharisees came to Jesus. They tried to make him say something wrong. They asked him, "Is it right for a man to divorce his wife for any reason he chooses?" Jesus answered, "Surely you have read this in the Scriptures: When God made the world, 'he made people male and female.' And God said, 'That is why a man will leave his father and mother and be joined to his wife. And the two people will become one.' So they are no longer two, but one. God has joined them together, so no one should separate them." The Pharisees asked, "Then why did Moses give a command allowing a man to divorce his wife by writing a certificate of divorce?" Jesus answered, "Moses allowed you to divorce your wives because you refused to accept God's teaching. But divorce was not allowed in the beginning. I tell you that whoever divorces his wife, except for the problem of sexual sin, and marries another woman is guilty of adultery" (***Matthew 19:3-9***).

What is friendship?

I give you a new command: Love each other. You must love each other just as I loved you. All people will know that you are my followers if you love each other (***John 13:34-35***). Forget about the wrong things people do to you. Don't try to get even. Love your neighbor as yourself. I am the Lord (***Leviticus 19:18***). You can trust what your friend says, even when it hurts. But your enemies want to hurt you, even when they act nice (***Proverbs 27:6***). Don't be friends with people who become angry easily. Don't stay around quick-tempered people. If you do, you may learn to be like them. Then you will have the same problems they do (***Proverbs 22:24-25***).

Your love must be real. Hate what is evil. Do only what is good. Love each other in a way that makes you feel close like brothers and sisters. And give each other more honor than you give yourself. As you serve the Lord, work hard and don't be lazy. Be excited about serving him! Be happy because of the hope you have. Be patient when you have troubles. Pray all the time. Share with God's people who need help. Look for people who need help and welcome them into your homes. Wish only good for those who treat you badly. Ask God to bless them, not curse them. When others are happy, you should be happy with them. And when others are sad, you should be sad too.

Live together in peace with each other. Don't be proud, but be willing to be friends with people who are not important to others. Don't think of yourself as smarter than everyone else. If someone does you wrong, don't try to pay them back by hurting them. Try to do what everyone thinks is right. Do the best you can to live in peace with everyone. My friends, don't punish anyone who does wrong to you. Wait for God to punish them with his anger. In the Scriptures the Lord says, "I am the one who punishes; I will pay people back." But you should do this: "If you have enemies who are hungry, give them something to eat. If you have enemies who are thirsty, give them something to drink. In doing this you will make them feel ashamed." Don't let evil defeat you, but defeat evil by doing good (***Romans 12:9-21***).

What is the power of the tongue?

When you talk, you should always be kind and wise. Then you will be able to answer everyone in the way you should (***Colossians 4:6***). Wise people always think before they speak, so what they say is worth listening to. Kind words are like honey; they are easy to accept and good for your health (***Proverbs 16:23-24***). Those who are good have good things saved in their hearts. That's why they say good things. But those who are evil have hearts full of evil, and that's why they say things that are evil. I tell you that everyone will have to answer for all the careless things they have said. This will happen on the day of judgment. Your words will be used to judge you. What you have said will show whether you are right or whether you are guilty (***Matthew 12:35-37***).

We all make many mistakes. A person who never said anything wrong would be perfect. Someone like that would be able to control their whole body too. We put bits into the mouths of horses to make them obey us. With these bits we can control their whole body. It is the same with ships. A ship is very big, and it is pushed by strong winds. But a very small rudder controls that big ship. And the one who controls the rudder decides where the ship will go. It goes where he wants it to go. It is the same with our tongue. It is a small part of the body, but it can boast about doing great things. A big forest fire can be started with only a little flame.

The tongue is like a fire. It is a world of evil among the parts of our body. It spreads its evil through our whole body and starts a fire that influences all of life. It gets this fire from hell. Humans have control over every kind of wild animal, bird, reptile, and fish, and they have controlled all these things. But no one can control the tongue. It is wild and evil, full of deadly poison. We use our tongues to praise our Lord and Father, but then we curse people who were created in God's likeness. These praises and curses come from the same mouth. My brothers and sisters, this should not happen. Do good water and bad water flow from the same spring? Of course not. My brothers and sisters, can a fig tree make olives? Or can a grapevine make figs? No, and a well full of salty water cannot give good water (***James 3:2-12***).

What is church?

The church is Christ's body. It is filled with him. He makes everything complete in every way (***Ephesians 1:23***). Yes, if two or three people are together believing in me, I am there with them (***Matthew 18:20***). We must not quit meeting together, as some are doing. No, we need to keep on encouraging each other. This becomes more and more important as you see the Day getting closer (***Hebrews 10:25***).

I hope I can come to you soon. But I am writing this to you now, so that, even if I cannot come soon, you will know how people should live in the family of God. That family is the church of the living God. And God's church is the support and foundation of the truth (***1 Timothy 3:14-15***).

What is tithing?

Jesus sat near the Temple collection box and watched as people put money into it. Many rich people put in a lot of money. Then a poor widow came and put in two very small copper coins, worth less than a penny. Jesus called his followers to him and said, "This poor widow put in only two small coins. But the truth is, she gave more than all those rich people. They have plenty, and they gave only what they did not need. This woman is very poor, but she gave all she had. It was money she needed to live on" (***Mark 12:41-44***). "People should not steal things from God, but you stole things from me." You say, 'What did we steal from you?' "You should have given me one-tenth of your things. You should have given me special gifts. In this way your whole nation has stolen things from me, so bad things are happening to you." The Lord All Powerful says, "Try this test. Bring one-tenth of your things to me. Put them in the treasury. Bring food to my house. Test me! If you do these things, I will surely bless you. Good things will come to you like rain falling from the sky. You will have more than enough of everything" (***Malachi 3:8-10***). Give this command to those who are rich with the things of this world. Tell them not to be proud. Tell them to hope in God, not their money. Money cannot be trusted, but God takes care of us richly. He gives us everything to enjoy.

Tell those who are rich to do good—to be rich in good works. And tell them they should be happy to give and ready to share. By doing this, they will be saving up a treasure for themselves. And that treasure will be a strong foundation on which their future life will be built. They will be able to have the life that is true life (***1 Timothy 6:17-19***). Don't save treasures for yourselves here on earth. Moths and rust will destroy them. And thieves can break into your house and steal them. Instead, save your treasures in heaven, where they cannot be destroyed by moths or rust and where thieves cannot break in and steal them. Your heart will be where your treasure is (***Matthew 6:19-21***). You cannot serve two masters at the same time. You will hate one and love the other, or you will be loyal to one and not care about the other. You cannot serve God and Money at the same time (***Matthew 6:24***).

How should I pray?

So this is how you should pray: 'Our Father in heaven, we pray that your name will always be kept holy. We pray that your kingdom will come—that what you want will be done here on earth, the same as in heaven. Give us the food we need for today. Forgive our sins, just as we have forgiven those who did wrong to us. Don't let us be tempted, but save us from the Evil One.' Yes, if you forgive others for the wrongs they do to you, then your Father in heaven will also forgive your wrongs. But if you don't forgive others, then your Father in heaven will not forgive the wrongs you do (***Matthew 6:9-15***).

How should I fast?

When you fast, don't make yourself look sad like the hypocrites. They put a look of suffering on their faces so that people will see they are fasting. The truth is, that's all the reward they will get. So when you fast, wash your face and make yourself look nice. Then no one will know you are fasting, except your Father, who is with you even in private. He can see what is done in private, and he will reward you in public. (***Matthew 6:16-18***).

How should I view my body?

"I am allowed to do anything," you say. My answer to this is that not all things are good. Even if it is true that "I am allowed to do anything," I will not let anything control me like a slave. Someone else says, "Food is for the stomach, and the stomach for food." Yes, and God will destroy them both. But the body is not for sexual sin. The body is for the Lord, and the Lord is for the body. And God will raise our bodies from death with the same power he used to raise the Lord Jesus.

Surely you know that your bodies are parts of Christ himself. So I must never take what is part of Christ and join it to a prostitute! The Scriptures say, “The two people will become one.” So you should know that anyone who is joined with a prostitute becomes one with her in body. But anyone who is joined with the Lord is one with him in spirit. So run away from sexual sin. It involves the body in a way that no other sin does. So if you commit sexual sin, you are sinning against your own body. You should know that your body is a temple for the Holy Spirit that you received from God and that lives in you. You don’t own yourselves. God paid a very high price to make you his. So honor God with your body (***1 Corinthians 6:12-20***).

Why did God send Jesus?

At one time you were separated from God. You were his enemies in your minds, because the evil you did was against him. But now he has made you his friends again. He did this by the death Christ suffered while he was in his body. He did it so that he could present you to himself as people who are holy, blameless, and without anything that would make you guilty before him.

And that is what will happen if you continue to believe in the Good News you heard. You must remain strong and sure in your faith. You must not let anything cause you to give up the hope that became yours when you heard the Good News. That same Good News has been told to everyone on earth, and that’s the work that I, Paul, was given to do (***Colossians 1:21-23***).

How can I please God?

Yes, the Scriptures say, "As surely as I live," says the Lord, "Everyone will bow before me; everyone will say that I am God." So each of us will have to explain to God about the things we do. So we should stop judging each other. Let's decide not to do anything that will cause a problem for a brother or sister or hurt their faith (***Romans 14:11-13***).

What does the Bible say about judging?

Don't judge others, and God will not judge you. If you judge others, you will be judged the same way you judge them. God will treat you the same way you treat others. Why do you notice the small piece of dust that is in your friend's eye, but you don't notice the big piece of wood that is in your own? Why do you say to your friend, 'Let me take that piece of dust out of your eye'? Look at yourself first! You still have that big piece of wood in your own eye. You are a hypocrite! First, take the wood out of your own eye. Then you will see clearly to get the dust out of your friend's eye (***Matthew 7:1-5***).

What does the Bible say about adultery?

Now, another man's wife might be very charming, and the words from her lips so sweet and inviting. But in the end, she will bring only bitterness and pain. It will be like bitter poison and a sharp sword. She is on a path leading to death, and she will lead you straight to the grave. Don't follow her. She has lost her way and does not even know it. Be careful. Stay on the road that leads to life.

Now, my sons, listen to me. Don't forget the words I say. Stay away from the woman who commits adultery. Don't even go near her house. If you do, others will get the honor you should have had. Some stranger will get everything you worked years to get. People you don't know will take all your wealth. Others will get what you worked for. At the end of your life, you will be sad that you ruined your health and lost everything you had. Then you will say, "Why didn't I listen to my parents? Why didn't I pay attention to my teachers? I didn't want to be disciplined. I refused to be corrected. So now I have suffered through just about every kind of trouble anyone can have, and everyone knows it (***Proverbs 5:3-14***).

How does God judge?

God is fair, and he will remember all the work you have done. He will remember that you showed your love to him by helping his people and that you continue to help them. We want each of you to be willing and eager to show your love like that the rest of your life. Then you will be sure to get what you hope for. We don't want you to be lazy. We want you to be like those who, because of their faith and patience, will get what God has promised. God made a promise to Abraham. And there is no one greater than God, so he made the promise with an oath in his own name—an oath that he would do what he promised.

He said, "I will surely bless you. I will give you many descendants." Abraham waited patiently for this to happen, and later he received what God promised. People always use the name of someone greater than themselves to make a promise with an oath. The oath proves that what they say is true, and there is no more arguing about it. God wanted to prove that his promise was true. He wanted to prove this to those who would get what he promised. He wanted them to understand clearly that his purposes never change. So God said something would happen, and he proved what he said by adding an oath. These two things cannot change: God cannot lie when he says something, and he cannot lie when he makes an oath. So these two things are a great help to us who have come to God for safety. They encourage us to hold on to the hope that is ours. This hope is like an anchor for us. It is strong and sure and keeps us safe. It goes behind the curtain. Jesus has already entered there and opened the way for us. He has become the high priest forever, just like Melchizedek (***Hebrews 6:10-20***).

What happens to people who don't experience a second birth?

But those who are cowards, those who refuse to believe, those who do terrible things, those who kill, those who sin sexually, those who do evil magic, those who worship idols, and those who tell lies—they will all have a place in the lake of burning sulfur. This is the second death (***Revelation 21:8***).

What happens to people who continue sinning?

If we decide to continue sinning after we have learned the truth, then there is no other sacrifice that will take away sins. If we continue sinning, all that is left for us is a fearful time of waiting for the judgment and the angry fire that will destroy those who live against God. Whoever refused to obey the Law of Moses was found guilty from the testimony given by two or three witnesses. Such people were not forgiven. They were killed.

So think how much more punishment people deserve who show their hate for the Son of God—people who show they have no respect for the blood sacrifice that began the new agreement and once made them holy or who insult the Spirit of God's grace. We know that God said, "I will punish people for the wrongs they do; I will repay them." And he also said, "The Lord will judge his people." It is a terrible thing to face punishment from the living God (***Hebrews 10:26-31***).

What is faith?

Faith is what makes real the things we hope for. It is proof of what we cannot see. God was pleased with the people who lived a long time ago because they had faith like this. Faith helps us understand that God created the whole world by his command. This means that the things we see were made by something that cannot be seen (***Hebrews 11:1-3***). Without faith no one can please God. Whoever comes to God must believe that he is real and that he rewards those who sincerely try to find him (***Hebrews 11:6***).

What does it mean to be called?

The Lord's message came to me: "Before I made you in your mother's womb, I knew you. Before you were born, I chose you for a special work. I chose you to be a prophet to the nations." Then I said, "But, Lord God, I don't know how to speak. I am only a boy." But the Lord said to me, "Don't say, 'I am only a boy.' You must go everywhere I send you and say everything I tell you to say. Don't be afraid of anyone. I am with you, and I will protect you." This message is from the Lord (***Jeremiah 1:4-8***).

How did Jesus respond to critics?

Jesus ate dinner at Matthew's house. Many tax collectors and others with bad reputations came and ate with him and his followers. The Pharisees saw that Jesus was eating with these people. They asked his followers, "Why does your teacher eat with tax collectors and other sinners?" Jesus heard them say this. So he said to them, "It is the sick people who need a doctor, not those who are healthy. You need to go and learn what this Scripture means: 'I don't want animal sacrifices; I want you to show kindness to people.' I did not come to invite good people. I came to invite sinners" (***Matthew 9:10-13***).

Does God favor the rich?

Jesus looked at the man in a way that showed how much he cared for him. He said, "There is still one thing you need to do. Go and sell everything you have. Give the money to those who are poor, and you will have riches in heaven. Then come and follow me." The man was upset when Jesus told him to give away his money. He didn't want to do this, because he was very rich. So he went away sad. Then Jesus looked at his followers and said to them, "It will be very hard for a rich person to enter God's

Kingdom!" The followers were amazed at what Jesus said. But he said again, "My children, it is very hard to enter God's Kingdom! It is easier for a camel to go through the eye of a needle than for a rich person to enter God's kingdom!" (***Mark 10:21-25***).

Is God rich?

Yes, God's riches are very great! His wisdom and knowledge have no end! No one can explain what God decides. No one can understand his ways. As the Scriptures say, "Who can know what is on the Lord's mind? Who is able to give him advice? Who has ever given God anything? God owes nothing to anyone." Yes, God made all things. And everything continues through him and for him. To God be the glory forever! Amen (***Romans 11:33-36***).

Why is companionship important?

Two people are better than one. When two people work together, they get more work done. If one person falls, the other person can reach out to help. But those who are alone when they fall have no one to help them. If two people sleep together, they will be warm. But a person sleeping alone will not be warm. An enemy might be able to defeat one person, but two people can stand back-to-back to defend each other. And three people are even stronger. They are like a rope that has three parts wrapped together—it is very hard to break (***Ecclesiastes 4:9-12***).

Part V – ASK

"We can come to God with no doubts. This means that when we ask God for things that agree with God, God cares about what we say. He listens every time we ask. He gives us whatever we ask of Him."

(1 John 5:15-15)

Answers to Common Questions

The previous section answered questions with direct quotes from the Bible. This section provides Bible-inspired answers. If you're confronted with a question that's not addressed, go to the Bible for the answer. If you're unable to locate or understand the answer, ask your discipler, pastor or spiritual leader for help. They'll gladly help you.

Does God love unbelievers?

Yes, God loves every single person on the planet, whether they believe in Him or not. There is absolutely nothing any one of us can do that will stop God's love. No way, no how. God simply loves us because we are His children. Although many of us have not accepted His son Jesus Christ into our hearts and are still far away from home, He continues to extend His love, mercy and grace so they will one day, finally, make it home.

Do you remember the thief on the cross who asked Jesus not to forget him when Jesus made it into Paradise? The complete story is in Luke 23. Well, when the thief asked Jesus to remember him, his heart went back home, just in the nick of time. It's never too late to come home. God is always waiting with open arms to receive all who have made the decision to come home. The decision to accept, believe and confess Jesus as our Lord and Savior, and give your heart a home, can only be made while you're alive. Once you are physically dead…well, that's another story. The bottom line is God loves us all.

Why do people hurt other people?

There are a lot of reasons why people hurt one another. Sometimes we're afraid of being vulnerable or experiencing physical, emotional or spiritual problems. Sometimes we feel sad or frustrated about life and lash out to diffuse the internal turmoil. This isn't right, but it happens, and it happens all too often. Until we are healed, people will continue to hurt people, especially those closest to them. This understanding should make us more empathic towards those who hurt others.

We should make an effort to continually pray for them until they are healed and whole. No matter how much others have hurt us, we should, like God, endeavor to show each other forgiveness, compassion, human love, kindness, respect, and consideration. If we believe God sent His son to die for all the hurt in this life, we must live according to the Word.

Why do bad things like floods, murder, and wars happen?

Bad things happen to bad people and bad things happen to good people. Most people blame God when various calamities occur in the world. You'll often hear them asking "Where was God when…?" Well God was there when things were perfect in the Garden of Eden and God is still here when things are 'not so perfect.' So even though Jesus Christ came to redeem the world from sin, we still live in an imperfect world. The Bible states that the world, which has not yet been redeemed, waits and groans for the second coming of the Lord, when all things will be once again made new. This is one mystery we will never be able to comprehend. So until then, bad things will happen to bad and good people alike. However, we continue to trust and rely upon the eternal God who gives us refuge and strength to overcome tragedies.

Is the devil real?

Yes, the devil is real. Many biblical scholars believe that the devil or Satan was once one of God's archangels. Lucifer, or "morning star," was a beautiful, brilliant and strong angel. As a matter of fact, he was the strongest and most beautiful creature in heaven. It's no wonder sin appears so attractive, enticing and overpowering at times. For whatever reason, most likely pride, he no longer wanted to obey God, he wanted to be worshipped by God. So he and other angels decided to fight against the all-powerful God. Bad idea. Because of their disobedience, God threw the devil and his co-conspirators out of heaven and right into earth. The devil awaits his final punishment at the end of the world, where he will be thrown into the lake of fire. In the meantime, the father of disobedience and the father of lies roams around the world like a roaring lion seeking to steal, kill and destroy lives. He tempts men and women to disobey and sin against God. Those who don't believe the devil is real cannot understand why seemingly nice people commit heinous and evil acts. But one thing's for sure, the devil can no longer be real in your life.

What will happen to me when I die?

If you're a believer in Jesus Christ, you have nothing to worry about when it comes to death. Death for believers is just a transport from one state of being into another. When your body dies, your spirit begins a brand new life in Heaven. Everything you know and enjoy in this life will come to a complete end at the time of death. When you arrive in heaven, your spirit will begin to enjoy the presence of the Lord in eternity.

As a believer, you have given your heart a home. Christ, your Savior and Lord, has prepared an eternal home for you in Heaven, a place where you and your new body will live forever. We're told the streets are paved with gold and there's no need for light, for Christ the Eternal Light is present. Many unbelievers, including agnostics and atheists, believe death is the complete end of life and nothing continues to exist in any other state or form. You know the truth. If we remain faithful to the end, we will live forever with God in Heaven. That's His word, and that's all we have for now is His word.

Do people have to die?

Yes, all living creatures die. Death is a reality we must confront and embrace. It's the natural course of life. Our mortal bodies are subject to decay, sickness, disease, and death and therefore cannot and will not live forever. We may never understand the mystery of death. After all, who can truly grasp the reality of losing a loved one without a moment's notice? But because we believe in Christ, and have Christ living inside us, we'll be resurrected in Him when we die. This is the hope we have in Him. We too will rise again.

Will it be difficult to share my testimony with others?

Yes, at first, it may be difficult to share your testimony. Even the most experienced believer will confess some degree of intimidation or shyness when sharing their faith. But we just need to share our faith. When we do something for God, the Bible instructs us to rely on Him. He will give us the strength and the confidence to tell others about Him. So when you share your faith, have confidence. He will be right there with you, guiding and leading your words and actions in every situation. Don't be shy. Don't be afraid. Describe your life before you met Christ and compare it to your life now. That's your story. No one can ever deny that. Let people know how much He loves us all and wants to be a part of our lives. If the person you're speaking with is ready to receive Christ, don't hesitate to lead them in the sinner's prayer or the prayer of salvation. Both prayers are found in Part VI—PRAY of this book. But if the person isn't ready, don't be offended. Know that God used you in a profound way to open the door of their heart and sow the seed of His Word. In time, He will, as He did for you and I, revisit their lives and expose them to His love.

Can Christians have fun?

Absolutely. By no means is Christianity boring. I don't know of anything more exciting than being free from the bondage of sin, sickness and death. We have the peace of God and the Holy Spirit as a constant companion and guide. This is the greatest knowing EVER! Because we know this, believers are happy and joyous people, enjoying the abundant life here and now. Okay, so we don't get drunk, party all night, sleep around, and a whole bunch of other stuff anymore, but that's our choice. Plus, those things never truly satisfied us anyway. Because we love God so much, we don't wish to do anything that displeases Him. We enjoy and participate in some social activities that unbelievers enjoy, but in a different way. We go to concerts, movies, parties, plays, family gatherings, sporting events, cruises, vacations, and just about everything, always mindful that what we say and do must always please and glorify God.

What does it mean to fellowship?

Fellowship is time spent with those who believe in Jesus, "Yes, if two or three people are together believing in me, I am there with them" (Matthew 18:20). It's such an awesome experience. You can share what you love, learn about Jesus, pray with and for one another, and even laugh and cry together. You see, Christ not only brought us back into a relationship with God, He also united us all into His body. Christ is in the midst of all our fellowships, saving, healing, restoring, caring, and loving us all. He's the one who binds our hearts and spirits together. All that He is and desires to be in us will be known to those who come together in His name. Therefore, it's important we fellowship with those who also believe in Jesus.

What does it mean to be "born again"?

Nicodemus, a Jewish church elder, asked Jesus the same question. How can one be born again if they're old and unable to re-enter the womb of their mother? That's a good question Nicodemus. I would've asked the same question. But Jesus, when He spoke of a second birth, He wasn't speaking of a physical birth, like Nicodemus thought, He was speaking of a spiritual birth. Allow me to explain. Your birthday marks the day you came into the world. That was the first time you were born. Now, no matter how cute you were as a child, you had the nature of sin bubbling inside. As a child, you unknowingly told lies and, at times, you were mean and unkind to other children. You couldn't help yourself. You were a sinner. We all were. We were in desperate need of a Savior. That's why God sent Jesus Christ, His only son, into the world to die on the cross for our sins. When we accept Him into our heart, we experience a second birth, a spiritual birth. This is the birth Jesus spoke of in John 3:3, "I assure you, everyone must be born again. Anyone who is not born again cannot be in God's kingdom." You have been born again, spiritually born, when you accept Jesus as your Lord and Savior. Do you remember Saul of Tarsus who was introduced in the Book of Acts? Well he hated Christians so much he spent all his time and energy making sure they were punished or killed for their faith. But he ultimately gave his heart to the Lord and was born again after a bright light from heaven appeared to him on his way to Damascus. He prayed and fasted for three consecutive days until he was filled with the Holy Spirit. His name was changed to Paul the Apostle, and despite being responsible for countless deaths, he became known as the greatest theologian and pastor of all times. So remember, no matter how heinous or wicked a person is, they too can receive Christ's love into their heart. It's never too late to be born again.

What is the difference between a pastor, priest and bishop?

They pretty much do the same thing. They're all God's appointed and anointed servants. They have a responsibility from God to care for the spiritual growth of the members of their congregations. They teach and preach the Word of God, counsel those in need, pray for the emotional and physical welfare of their members, organize spiritually uplifting activities, perform wedding and burial ceremonies, and appoint gifted leaders to manage other church affairs.

They often attend graduation ceremonies, weddings and birthday celebrations of their members. Because they watch over God's flock, the church, we're required by God to pray for them. They're human just like you and I so they're bound to make mistakes and be confronted with the same things as us. During difficult times, pray for them and ask God to show you how you can be a blessing to their lives.

Why do we sing at worship service?

Whenever you're overjoyed or excited, you generally burst out in laughter or song right? You don't care who's watching you, even if you sound awful, you have to let it all out. Praising and worshipping God in hymns and songs is pretty much the same thing. Singing is our way of showing God how much we love Him and how grateful we are for what He does in our lives. When the ark of the Lord entered the City of David, King David broke out in a song and dance (***2 Samuel 6***). He sang and praised God so much his outer garments fell off.

Oops! His daughter was embarrassed, but he wasn't. He loved to worship God. In fact, King David wrote most of the songs in the book of Psalms. He knew how to praise God, he not only sang praises when he was happy, he also sang praises when he was sad. He praised God no matter what. Don't be embarrassed or shy to openly praise God, praise Him and sing along.

What does it mean to baptize?

Baptism is our way of showing the world we belong to the Lord. It shows we've given our hearts to the Lord and are proud of being identified with Him. Baptism is important to Jesus. It's how he began His public ministry. It was while He was being baptized, dipped in the River Jordan by John the Baptist, that the Holy Spirit descended on Him like a dove and a voice from Heaven declared, "This is my Son, the one I love. I am very pleased with him" (***Matthew 3:17***).

Jesus set an example for us to follow. Before Christ's ascension into Heaven, He instructed His disciples, "So go and make followers of all people in the world. Baptize them in the name of the Father and the Son and the Holy Spirit" (***Matthew 28:19***). Believers all over the world are baptized in pools, rivers, ponds, oceans, and just about anywhere water is available. Baptism is such a wonderful and spiritual experience.

You shouldn't be afraid of being baptized or concerned that you won't remain faithful to God after you're baptized. Believers who've put off baptism because they want to fix everything in their lives before they make a public declaration find they'll never get it right until they commit to Him. We should put all our trust in the Lord, commit to Him, and follow His example. Go ahead and be baptized.

Is a church a building?

No, a church is not a building. Anywhere Christians gather to pray, praise, fellowship, and worship the Lord is a church. In fact, God promised it only takes two people gathered in His name for Him to show up and be in the midst. So a church is not a building and God is not concerned with how many people show up. As long as there are at least two people praising God, it's considered a church. The physical place doesn't make a difference. Christians all over the world gather in homes, hotels, schools, auditoriums, huts, under a tree, or in tents to praise and worship the Lord.

So much emphasis has been placed on going to a building that we miss the true essence of who we are as the body of Christ—the church. We should make it a point of duty to regularly get together with other believers to worship, pray and praise God together.

Are there still miracles happening today?

Yes! Miracles are one of the ways in which God shows His love to the world. Miracles are not magic or tricks, they're real. The same power God gave His son Jesus to heal the sick, help the hopeless, and raise the dead is available to believers today. Anyone who has faith in Jesus will be able to do as He did. No coincidence or luck is involved, just your faith in God. Faith, not your feelings, moves God to produce the opportunities for miracles. Have faith in miracles and see what happens in your life.

How can believers help people who need help?

There is always someone in need. God will speak to you and

let you know whom He desires you to help or bless through your life. Listen to Him and respond. Your life is a treasured gift from God. You may show your appreciation for His gift of life by loving those whom He loves and helping those in need.

You're God's hands, eyes and heart extended in the world. He wants to use you to love and bless others. When you reach out to help those in need, you're putting your faith in action. You're letting God know you believe He's in your life, that He loves you, has blessed you, and will use you to love and bless others.

What are Christians known for?

Believers in Jesus Christ are known for leading people to the Lord, sharing the gospel of Christ and helping people. In fact, many caring organizations in the world are Christian-based, such as Goodwill and Habitat for Humanity. Christians have opened up many orphanages to care for those who've lost their parents, adoption agencies to unite children with loving parents, nursing and retirement homes to care for the sick and the elderly, and food pantries to feed the homeless and needy. Christians also send care packages to people serving in prison or the military. Believers are strategically placed all around the world to extend God's love to all people, whether they believe in God or not.

This is most evident in times of immense tragedy, crisis, or unfathomed calamity. There is always a need for volunteers and monetary contributions. That's where you and I come in. We can also be a part of what God is doing throughout the world by volunteering our services, contributing monies and sending care packages to these organizations. They're always in need. And it's the right thing to do, the God thing to do. Ask God in prayer which group or organization He wants you to support so you fulfill His will and not your own.

What does God call sin?

Sin is anything that separates us from God. All sins are equal; there is no such thing as a big sin or a small sin. We should never be comfortable with sin. Christ in His death on the cross took a hold of sin and dealt with it once and for all. Sin no longer has any power over us. Yet if you sin, you can always go to our Heavenly Father in prayer and ask Him for His forgiveness. If you have a sincere desire to change, He will offer forgiveness and give you strength to overcome sin. When we overcome sin in certain areas, we should be helpful to those who have not arrived.

Who is the Holy Spirit?

The Holy Spirit ('pneuma' in Greek) is the breath of God. The age of the Holy Spirit is from the Day of Pentecost until the second return of Christ. Unfortunately, the personality, empowerment, works, and gifts of the Holy Spirit are misunderstood and misused. Because of the varying symbolisms associated with the Holy Spirit, such as oil and water, many believers view the Holy Spirit as a mere influence, when in reality, the Holy Spirit is a Divine person.

One must come to a clear understanding of who He is to appreciate the work, person and ministry of the Holy Spirit. He is God and as God, true worship and reverence must be given to Him.

He not only empowers, He desires to possess our lives. He communicates to and through the person He possesses. He seeks to guide and lead the believer into all truth and to comfort him, as He is the Wonderful Comforter. He has a mind, will and a full range of emotions. Our advocate, as He is often called, performs various acts. He convicts men of truth, reveals the will of God and brings illumination to His Word.

This blessed and glorious privilege of having the power of the Godhead dwelling in our mortal bodies should bring continuous joy. We must come to the knowledge that, as the active agent in the life of the believer, the Holy Spirit is God, the Son of God, and was with the Son before all things were created. As God, He possesses the same essential and moral attributes. He is omnipresent, omniscient and an eternal life source.

At the point of conversion, the Holy Spirit baptizes us. This speaks of the permanent indwelling of all believers. He is a gift to all believers. He secures and authenticates the work of Christ in our lives by imprinting our spirit with Himself. We as believers must make ourselves flexible to the volition of the Holy Spirit who is in and upon us.

As we submit our spirit to His presence, we will find Him to be a producer of Christ-like character, imparter and leader of life, giver of calling and assurance, the anointer for service, strengthener of being, and the enabler of prayers. Our Savior Jesus Christ was born of the Spirit, filled with His fullness, led by the Spirit, empowered, and anointed by the Spirit. Believers should seek to experience His fullness in their lives, for without the Holy Spirit, there is no life.

Why did Jesus die?

Jesus died so we could live. You see, a long, long, time ago, a few days after God created the world, heaven and the earth, light and darkness, night and day, land and sea, sun and moon, He made two perfect human beings, Adam and Eve, and placed them in His beautiful garden, the Garden of Eden. Adam and Eve had everything their hearts could ever desire. They got along well with the animals and enjoyed a wonderful and intimate relationship with God who walked and talked with them in the garden each day. They were made in the image of God so they would never get sick or die. They would live forever. Life was great. God gave them everything they needed and told them they could eat from all the trees in His beautiful garden, except from the tree of the knowledge of good and evil.

Then the devil, who was already cast out of heaven and into the earth, paid Adam and Eve a visit in the Garden of Eden. The devil deceived Eve by telling her if she ate of the tree of knowledge, she would not die, but become as wise as God, knowing good and evil. Eve believed what he said and ate of the fruit. She also gave the fruit to Adam to eat. By doing so, they both disobeyed God and everything that was once beautiful and perfect got really, really ugly. Sin, sickness and death entered the world. God, in His mercy and love, promised them He would send His 'seed,' His son Jesus Christ, to pay the ultimate price for the sins of the world. God kept his promise. Two thousand years ago God gave His only son to the world that whosoever believe in Him would not perish but have life everlasting. So why did Jesus die? He died to save us from our sins, to bring us back into a relationship with God, and to give us eternal life.

Why should I tithe (give money) to the church?

To tithe is to give a tenth of what you earn to God. Tithing is an Old and New Testament command, yet people still question whether they should tithe. The children of Israel, God's chosen people, were commanded to give a tithe of their grain, fruit, herd, flock, produce, or income to the Lord. They would do this to acknowledge and celebrate the abundance of God's provision, support the maintenance of God's church (not just the building, but the family of God) and provide for the poor. Believers in Jesus Christ today have an obligation to tithe. In love and appreciation for what God does for us and in us, we should tithe our time, energy and money. We should invest our lives and possessions into the kingdom of God. If you find it difficult to give to God who is the giver and sustainer of life, ask the Holy Spirit to show you what's in your heart that won't let you give to the one who gives you life. He will show you your heart. He will show you when, where and how much to invest. Tithing lets God know we appreciate and celebrate His provision for our lives. It demonstrates we trust He'll continue to meet our needs, answer our prayers, and continue to give us His best. He already gave us His only son Jesus. Therefore, it should be easy for us to tithe. He's not asking for a whole lot, just a tenth. He said test Him, try Him, and He'll give us a return we won't have room for. Whatever you give Him, He'll take it, bless it and give it back to you a hundred times over. You will never be able to out-give God, tithe out of love for God and see for yourself.

Part VI— PRAY

"When people do not listen to God's teachings,
he does not listen to their prayers"
(**Proverbs 29:8**).

What is prayer?

Prayer is intimate dialogue between God and his people. It's an opportunity for you, individually or collectively, to speak with God. But prayer isn't just about talking to God; it's about listening to Him too.

Consider prayer a two-way conversation between you and God. When you talk to God, He listens. Then, when God talks to you, you listen. Sometimes you may find yourself doing all the talking while God listens. Other times God may be doing all the talking while you listen.

Whether you're doing the talking or the listening, God is always available to you, 24 hours a day, 7 days a week. Bring your cares, questions, burdens, needs, fears, battles, struggles, wants, thoughts, victories, and desires to God. Then, be patient. God always responds.

Why does God want me to pray?

God wants you to pray because He wants you to have a personal and intimate relationship with Him. Prayer is just one of the ways in which you can draw closer to Him. The more time you spend with Him in prayer, the more you'll know and love Him. God loves you. In fact, He loves you so much, He sent His Son to prove His love.

To experience His love, all you have to do is pray. Prayer keeps your love tank full and your burden baskets light. It helps you refocus your attention on the One who knows the beginning and end of all things. Prayer helps realign your life with the will and purpose of God.

Why say "in Jesus' name" in prayer?

Christians say "In Jesus' name" because they're responding to what Jesus said to his Disciples, "If you ask me for anything in my name, I will do it" (***John 14:14***). It's a believer's way of letting God know you believe in His Son Jesus Christ and have placed all your trust in Him.

God still wants you to mean what you say when you pray, so using the words "In Jesus' name" is not enough. More than words, God wants you to be sincere with Him and mean it when you pray 'In Jesus name.' There is no other name by which we can be saved.

And get this…even demons tremble at the name of Jesus.

Now that's powerful. God has given us a name that is above any other name, so let's use it and pray in the name of Jesus.

Why say "amen" to end prayer?

The word 'amen' means yes, it is certain, or so be it. Believers say amen at the end of all prayers to let God know our prayers are true and sincere. If we're certain our prayer is according to His will, He will bring it to pass. When we say amen, we believe God's heard our prayers and He'll answer. Amen!

Will God answer my prayers?

God promises to answer our prayers if the prayers are asked according to His will, not ours. Apply God's principles and your prayers will be answered. As a matter of fact, you'll begin to anticipate answers because your prayers will be within the realm of his will. As soon as you make prayer a part of your daily lifestyle, your life will change.

Prayer in its proper order yields perfect results. However, you must remember this: prayer is always activated by faith. Prayer does not cause faith to work; faith causes prayer to work. You must first believe He is God. Then, when your faith is in Him and Him alone, He will prove no other God or Lord can compare to Him.

Why are my prayers unanswered?

Many people are unaware of the obstacles hinder a prayer life. To see the obstacles in your own prayer life, honestly and humbly ask the Lord to show them to you.

Below are six common obstacles to prayer:

1. **Wrong motives**

   When asking God for something, check your motives. He already knows what you want and why you want it. He's God, remember, He made you so He knows your motives before you do. Be honest with yourself about your prayer motives.

2. **Praying out of God's will**

   Always be in agreement with God. The Bible helps discern God's will in any situation. If your prayers line up with God's will, He will never hold back the answer you desire.

3. **Impure heart**

   The Lord will not hear your prayers if you have evil in your heart. If Jesus is the Lord of your life and is the ultimate authority over all your decisions, your heart will be pure. As a believer, confess your sin to the Lord, repent, and ask that the rich and powerful blood of our savior cleanse that sin. God will listen and respond. When you're in agreement with God's son, you're in agreement with the Father.

4. **Failing to get quiet before the Lord**

   You and God can't talk at the same time. Learn to listen to God.

While you're talking, He's listening. You should be fair and listen too. There are a lot of people who never listen. I once heard a gentleman say, "If all you do is talk, you know nothing but yourself." Those who don't listen to people don't listen to God either. They might say, "Listen Lord, I'm talking right now." They don't let God speak so they walk away from prayer the same way they came in—confused. We have to practice being still before the Lord. That means we should get before the Lord, humble ourselves, and say, "Lord, speak to your servant. I'm listening to you. I know nothing." Maybe He wants to tell you how He'll answer your prayer and how you should prepare yourself. He won't force you to listen. He wants you to listen with a willful heart. God isn't a bully; He'll wait patiently. After all, He has all the time in the world, but do you?

5. ***Not making prayer a daily habit***

You need prayer just like you need food and water. Without food and water, you die. Similarly, without prayer, you're spiritually dead. In the business of life, the enemy of your soul will make you think you don't have time to pray every day. You make excuses and start your day off without God or prayer. When you do this, you're telling yourself you don't need God because you're in full control of your life. This makes the enemy's job easy. Prayer does not have to be two or three hours a day. If that's your goal and you achieve it, great, but quantity does not mean quality.

In fact, more can be accomplished in a 10-minute sincere prayer than an obligated hour-long prayer. Ultimately, whether you pray a few minutes or a few hours, God is pleased to hear from you. God can talk to everybody at the same time. He can hold the world in one hand and you in the other. You can talk to Him anytime. It's all up to you. But remember, prayer is not a choice; it's a command. To fulfill God's purpose, communion with God daily.

6. **Unforgiveness**

   Trust God when He says you must forgive. He has a plan in His law that blesses those who forgive. Be like Jesus; forgive and love your perpetrators. If you don't, the unforgiveness in your heart will fester into something worse than the initial offense. You'll build up the same resentment and bitterness they had and it'll become a vicious cycle. Unforgiveness has its own spirit, and if you carry it around, it makes you sick and miserable. At some time, you hurt someone, don't you want to be forgiven? If there's anyone you haven't forgiven, let God know the weaknesses you have in dealing with that person. Let Him know your desire to please Him and your willingness to forgive. God makes true forgiveness possible, ask for His help.

What should I do before prayer?

Before praying, you must be honest about your reasons for prayer. God already knows your motives, but do you? To develop a prayer life pleasing to God, you must understand a prayer life unpleasing to God. One of the biggest hindrances to a successful prayer life is dishonesty. After all, if you can't be honest with yourself, you'll never be honest with God. Answer these questions honestly before prayer and your motives will reveal themselves to you:

1. What is my prayer goal?
2. Does my prayer goal line up with God's will for my life?

3. Am I willing to change my prayer goal to please God?
4. Does this prayer benefit me only?
5. Does this prayer allow someone to suffer or be punished?
6. How long am I willing to wait to hear God's answer to my prayer?
7. Will I accept God's answers even if they're not pleasing to me?
8. Will the answer to my prayer win a soul or make me a better witness for the Lord?
9. Have I asked God what He wants from me?
10. Have I forgiven my brother or sister before prayer?

What are daily prayer principles?

Today's fast-paced lifestyles demand relief and that relief is found in prayer. Countless people are hurting from personal disappointments, broken families, lost friendships, distant spouses, and financial stresses. Prayer is the only answer to address such difficulties. The author of our being, the preserver of our life, the one who formed us in His own divine image will provide for our necessities if we trust in Him. His word is true. Follow these daily prayer principles and witness the changes in your life:

1. **Schedule time**
   Set aside time each day for prayer and Bible study. It's best when you first wake up. There are usually less distractions, your mind is fresh and most importantly, God will help plan your day.

2. **Speak simply and naturally**
   Tell God any and everything on your mind. I assure you He's listening. Talk the way you talk. You don't need to be formal

or say fancy spiritual words and phrases. Talk to God in any language. He made you, He understands you. Thank Him and praise Him for all He's done in your life and thank Him for what He's going to do. Praise Him for who He is, not for what He can do for you. Tell God you'll listen to Him.

3. **Be grateful**

   Thank God for your life, for your last inhale, your last exhale. Thank God for everything you've experienced and will experience. Thank God for your food, shelter and clothing. Thank God for your friends and family. Thank God for your struggles. Thank God for your successes. Thank God for everything. He's listening.

4. **Ask questions**

   Ask God if there's unrepented sin in your life. If there is, ask God to help you fix them. Ask God to help with your most pressing concerns. Ask Him to show you times when He wanted to answer your prayer, but you weren't ready. Let Him know you're ready to hear the truth, even if it hurts. Ask and he'll respond.

5. **Be selfless**

   Affirm to God your prayer is selfless by praying for your enemies. This is a hard one, but God requires it for you to be blessed. Besides, it shows God you want to be like His son Jesus. Think of how God can be glorified if you pray for your enemies. Always hope that the answer to your prayer leads someone to accept Jesus into his or her life. Ask Him to surround the world and your loved ones with His mercy, grace and unconditional love. Ask him to help neighbors, colleagues and friends; request for others what you request for yourself.

6. **Prioritize God**

   Always let God know you accept His will over your own personal desires. Remember, He knows your heart's desires and your true motives. Prioritize His will over yours and you'll be blessed.

7. **Pray for the intangible**

   Pray for power, strength, courage, confidence, hope, peace, love, forgiveness, patience, wisdom, and understanding. You'll need them all. These tools will release a tremendous power in you and give you the boldness to face a world that's dying daily because of its moral decay, pride and selfishness.

8. **Pray for abundance**

   God has an unlimited amount of resources. Our human minds could never imagine the ways He's capable of blessing us. Don't limit God by your thinking. Remind yourself of God's power and pray for abundance. With that abundance, ask for humility to handle the abundance.

9. ***Pray for our leaders***

   In every prayer, pray for the leaders of this nation and its moral stand. Pray for the ministries that share the Gospel of Jesus to the world. Pray for those feeding the hungry, giving shelter to the homeless, building water wells, adopting children, and providing health, medicine and love.

Pray for local communities, churches, law enforcement officials, public health administrators, and non-profit and charitable organizations that are in line with God's will and purpose. Pray for them and the well-being of their loved ones.

Daily communion with God teaches precious lessons, dissolves anxious thoughts, and replaces fears and worries with joy and peace. Through daily prayer filled with faith, God provides wisdom, vision, provision, and answered prayers. Each time you pray, remember that God, rich in love, grace, mercy, kindness, and forgiveness, will answer any request pleasing to Him.

What is the Lord's Prayer?

To please God, you must converse with Him in prayer the way Jesus instructed the disciples. These instructions are commonly referred to as the Lord's Prayer. Each Bible version has a slightly different account of The Lord's Prayer. Below is the Easy-to-Read Version of The Lord's Prayer, along with an explanation of each sentence:

Our Father in heaven, we pray that your name will always be kept holy. We pray that your kingdom will come—that what you want will be done here on earth, the same as in heaven. Give us the food we need for today. Forgive our sins, just as we have forgiven those who did wrong to us. Don't let us be tempted, but save us from the Evil One (***Matthew 6:9-13***). Amen.

1. Our Father in heaven, we pray that your name will always be kept holy. We're acknowledging three things: God resides in

Heaven, we want God to be praised and honored by people all over the world, and that God is holy, which means "set apart."

2. We pray that your kingdom will come—that what you want will be done here on earth, the same as in heaven.
   We want God's kingly rule to come so every knee will bow before Christ and people on earth will obey God's will just as the angels in heaven obey.
3. Give us the food we need for today.
   We're asking God to feed us His word so we can enjoy what He has in store for us.

4. Forgive our sins, just as we have forgiven those who did wrong to us.
   We're asking God to pardon our sins against Him as He makes us able to pardon what others have done to us.

5. Don't let us be tempted, but save us from the Evil One.
   We're asking God to protect us in tempting situations and from the enemy.

6. Amen. We're agreeing with God that He answers.

What is the Prayer of Salvation?

If you've never accepted Jesus as your Lord and Savior, now's a wonderful opportunity to do so. With the Prayer of Salvation, God erases everything you've done wrong in your entire life. He promises to forgive and forget if you believe in Him. I don't know about you, but I've never been offered anything better. So, as you can probably guess, I accepted Jesus as my Lord and Savior and since then, my life's never been the same. It can be that easy for you too. Here's how easy it was for me:

Jesus, thank you for dying on the cross for my sins. I want to know who You are right now. You said whoever believes in You shall not perish, but live forever with You. Well Jesus, I believe in You. I confess I'm a sinner and in need of a Savior right now. I believe You're the Savior you say you are. I believe You are the Son of God. I thank You for paying a price I could never pay and ask you to forgive me for the sins I've committed and will commit against You. Right now I ask You to come into my life and cleanse me with Your blood. I want to turn away from what the Bible calls sin. Fill me with your Holy Spirit. It's hard for me to comprehend or even imagine a love so great so I'm going to need your help, to love You, serve You, and obey You. I want to be born again. Make me a new creation .I want to live with you in eternity. Jesus, if You do this for me I will serve You, honor You, and follow You all the days of my life. Thank you for not giving up on me. You no longer have to wait for me. I'm coming after you now. Your dying on the cross will not be in vain for me. Today I give you my heart, my mind, my body and my soul forever. I ask this in Jesus' name. AMEN.

What is a Rededication Prayer?

When I was 13 years old, I was baptized. I had no idea what that really meant. Then, on April 22, 2001, after much pain and disappointment, I gave my life back to Jesus, never to leave Him again. That day, I rededicated my life to Jesus. Below is my rededication prayer, stating how much I love Him. If you've left the Lord before and want to come back home, He's waiting for your rededication prayer. Please, say this prayer with sincerity and come back home:

Father in Heaven, I know you are the God of second chances and new beginnings. I have let you down. I now realize you love me more than I can ever imagine. I also know you sent your one and only unique son to die on the cross for me. It's taken some time, but I'm getting the picture now, loud and clear. I know I'm not what you purposed me to be yet, but this time I'm on my way. Fill me with your Holy Spirit and forgive me for walking away from the only thing in this life that can save me from this life. Thank you Father for your forgiveness I'm so sorry for not listening to you and obeying your Word. I lied to you and broke my promise, but you've kept your word. And I now know that compared to your forgiveness, love, mercy, and grace, this world has nothing it could offer me to make me turn my back on you again.

Thank you for not leaving me or forsaking me as I have you. Thank you for allowing me the chance to come home again. This time I won't leave. But I need your help today. I realize I can't do this on my own. So today I re-dedicate my life to you and your purpose for me…never to walk away again. Once again I make you my savior and the Lord of my life. I've cleaned out my heart and my life to make room for you and I humbly welcome you back in my heart and into my life. My heart now has a home. I ask this in Jesus' name. AMEN.

What Is A Disciple's Prayer?

The day I became a disciple, I wanted to dedicate a prayer to God to show my faithfulness. Here is that prayer.

Father in Heaven, you gave Jesus to me, not only as a redeemer but also as a model. In Him I can see what it means to love you with everything in me. Your one and only unique Son lived each moment as an example to us all. He lived his entire life as an act of love dedicated to you. He played to an audience of One. And in every challenge with all He faced, He embraced nothing but your Holy will. He trusted you fully and because of His trust in you, His time on this earth was a continual act of self-sacrifice. He was the first disciple. So Father, with my whole heart I humbly ask that you allow me to imitate this great example of love so unselfishly that I offer you my complete love as He did. With your help, I will never again turn my back on you regardless of what I face or how I feel. Father, do with me as you wish.

This day I proclaim with my whole heart that you take and receive all my liberty, my understanding and my will. This life I have was given to me by you. Today I return back to you and surrender it entirely to be governed by your will. Your servant needs only your love and your grace. With these I am rich enough and ask for nothing more. Father, keep me focused on the glory you promised to those who love and obey you. Help me to share the news of this gospel to a world who wants to ignore Your place on the cross and what it represents to all of our lives. Father, using your word and the testimony of those who have come before me, help me to fill the wards of your Kingdom with souls in numbers unimagined. And never allow my will to have presence as long as your will exists. Father, allow me to be your disciple just like the Son of your greatest glory. And this day I proclaim "NOT MY WILL BUT YOURS BE DONE!"

IN JESUS NAME I PRAY, AMEN!

Final Thoughts—LOVE

"We should think about each other to see how we can encourage each other to show love and do good works. We must not quit meeting together, as some are doing. No, we need to keep on encouraging each other.
This becomes more and more important as you see the Day getting closer"
(**Hebrews 10:24-15**).

We've all faced the fear of failure, pain and rejection, but God has equipped His children with the necessary tools for replacing fear with love. John reminds the believer that love is the only weapon that can destroy fear, "So we know the love that God has for us, and we trust that love. God is love. Everyone who lives in love lives in God, and God lives in them (***1 John 4:16-17***). Whenever fear is present we should draw on the power of God's love within that is greater than any external force that divides us. Evict fear once and for all by choosing to love.

As you begin to place your life under the microscopic power of the Word and truly allow the Holy Spirit to be your guide, change will occur in your relationships with God, your neighbor, the enemy, and fellow believers.

Relationship with God: God speaks to us in His Word. Whatever He asks you to do, no matter how difficult it may seem, remember God has equipped you to do it. Many have experienced the painful consequence of not doing exactly what God says and have lived to regret it. Nevertheless, God gives us mercy and strength so we get it right the next time around. Do what He asks the first time; it's a lot easier.

Relationship with Believers: Your church family is made up of individuals just like you, and in fact, many have been where you are in life right now. The Bible encourages us to fellowship with other believers to pray, study, and obey God's Word. Together, we can bask in the fellowship of His love. We need each other on this Christian journey.

Relationship with Neighbors: You will be given countless opportunities to show the love of God to those you meet. The question is, what will you do? Some of those you help will be unkind, bitter, mean, and angry. They may laugh, curse, and even abuse you. Will you stop helping? No! Your daily reading of the Word will show you exactly what to do. It will show you how to love, forgive, be kind, patient, show compassion, and be gentle in your relationships.

Relationship with the Enemy: The devil or Satan has no need to bother, tempt, or fight against those who are already serving him. It's you, the believer that he's truly after. This is not meant to scare you, but to keep you on your guard. The enemy will use things, people, and situations to tempt, seduce, and entice you to do that which is evil in the sight of the Lord. He may even use your own family and friends so get ready to resist him. God shows you in His Word how He protects, defends and fights for you.

Relationship with Self: We often see the small piece of dust in our friend's eye and not notice the log that is in our own" (***Matthew 7:3-5***). Before casting blame and speaking unkind words, pause and consider the log in your own eyes. Often times, the fault we find in another person may be a result of the conflicts you avoid within yourself. Things like un-forgiveness, faithlessness, prayerlessness, selfishness, and disobedience must be replaced by love. Commit your weaknesses and shortcomings to God. In doing so, you may no longer see the speck that was in your friend's eyes.

As a believer, you must be on guard at all times and wear the spiritual armor of God. The sixth and final chapter of Ephesians explains this in great detail:

To end my letter I tell you, be strong in the Lord and in his great power. Wear the full armor of God. Wear God's armor so that you can fight against the devil's clever tricks. Our fight is not against people on earth. We are fighting against the rulers and authorities and the powers of this world's darkness. We are fighting against the spiritual powers of evil in the heavenly places. That is why you need to get God's full armor. Then on the day of evil, you will be able to stand strong. And when you have finished the whole fight, you will still be standing (***Ephesians 6:10-13***).

This is no 'super-hero' garb you can put on and take off at your own convenience. This is our divinely ordered, ever proven-armor of God. It keeps you super-charged spiritually and ready for anything. The Word will show you how God protects, delivers, defends, and fights for His children. God's word will also show you which enemy territories to avoid, the kind of battle it is, which weapons to use, when to engage the enemy, and when to stand and allow God to fight the battle for you.

You see, every battle is not yours to fight. Sometimes you may have to allow God to fight for you. You may have to remove yourself from certain toxic relationships and corrupt environments, which is even harder to do. Nevertheless, don't be afraid to fight the enemy. Go in with the power and strength of the Lord, use His weapons, and watch what God does. Here are reminders for your disciple ship journey to the Kingdom of Heaven:

- Have prayer daily with God. It's essential
- Read, study and apply God's word daily
- Obey God's word, regardless of how you feel
- Distinguish the distinct roles of God, Jesus and the Holy Spirit
- Invite the Holy Spirit to come upon you so you can receive his power
- Possess a teachable spirit; don't rebel and resist God's Word
- Attend and serve in a Bible-believing church that teaches and practices the Word of God
- Fellowship with other believers often
- Share your testimony as often as possible
- Be grateful to God for simple things
- Develop discernment in your daily decision-making
- Examine the true motives of your heart
- Read and reflect on Luke 14:25-33 the cost of discipleship
- Desire God's will over your own

- Endure ridicule, sacrifice, harassment, and hardship when sharing the Gospel with others
- Follow Jesus, even when it's unpopular or inconvenient
- Be willing to die for the cause of the gospel of Jesus Christ
- Learn the nature and habits of people so you can respond naturally and in love
- Above all else keep falling in love with Jesus

Destination Arrived

Just as you have been discipled, you must disciple others. Each one must teach one. We must make sure that those who come to the Lord never have a desire to leave.

It's been a pleasure journeying through the Word of God with you. I pray this book brings you closer to the Lord, and more importantly, I pray for your safe arrival to the Kingdom of Heaven. Stay close to your church family, they'll strengthen, nurture, guide, and encourage you in the faith. Your hope will always be in your intimate prayer life with God, and the knowledge of His word.

There will be days when you'll feel discouraged in your walk with the Lord. In that moment, pray to God and call your pastor, mentor, disciple, teacher, brother or sister in the Lord. Be honest with them. They'll pray for you, hold your hand and be a blessing to your life. God wants you to get some resolve; that's why godly people are in your life. James 5:16 says confess your sins to one another and pray for one another and you will be healed.

As you grow and mature in the things of God, it will be your turn to be there for someone else. Our Father in Heaven wants us all to love and help each other in every way because it shows His love. He wants us to think, act and talk in ways that honor Him. He wants all believers to disciple and love one another. In scripture, God gives us a way to measure our progress by his word saying "I give you a new command: Love each other. You must love each other just as I loved you. All people will know that you are my followers if you love each other" (***John 13:34-35***). If you're not loving your fellow brothers and sisters, get back to the drawing board and stay there until you do. This world is desperate for God and His love and we have both. Thank you for being open enough to allow me to share my heart with you. My prayer for all is that God blesses you and grants you your heart's deepest desires as you delight yourself in Him.

James Arceneaux Jr. grew up in Portland, Oregon. After attending the University of Oregon he moved to the Island of Hawaii. An interest in the entertainment business led him to Los Angeles. He worked in the industry for over 25 years with some of the top entertainers in the world. As a manger, estate manager, personal assistant and road manager he traveled the entire globe. In 2001 James rededicated his life to the Lord. During that time James began to have conversations with some new believers and realized that most of them were never discipled. Much like his own experience. That's when he discovered he had a heart for discipleship. Because of that alarming truth James made a personal vow to himself to write books, speak publically and make the discipleship of new believers the focus of his ministry and life.

Made in the USA
Middletown, DE
08 June 2023

31852190R00086